D1524120

The Devil Likes to Sing

For Cynthia,

Mary [illegible]

The Devil Likes to Sing

THOMAS J. DAVIS

For Cynthia—
All good wishes!
Nov. 2014

CASCADE *Books* • Eugene, Oregon

THE DEVIL LIKES TO SING

Cascade Books
An Imprint of Wipf and Stock Publishers
199 W. 8th Ave., Suite 3
Eugene, OR 97401

www.wipfandstock.com

ISBN 13: 978-1-61097-953-5

Cataloguing-in-Publication Data

Davis, Thomas J. (Thomas Jeffery), 1958–

The devil likes to sing / Thomas J. Davis

vi + 138 p. ; 23 cm.

ISBN 13: 978-1-61097-953-5

1. Devil—fiction. 2. Good and evil—fiction. 3. Devil in literature. 4. Temptation—Religious aspects—Christianity. I. Title.

PS3616.O63 D38 2014

Manufactured in the U.S.A.

My thanks to those who encouraged me along the way—friends who patiently listened to me talk about the "devil" book (and especially Philip Goff, who always laughed at the right places) and readers whose positive words kept me going.

"The devil prowls around like a roaring lion looking for someone to devour."

1 PETER 5:8

"The devil . . . is a liar and the father of lies."

JOHN 8:44

All is not lost; the unconquerable Will,
And study of revenge, immortal hate,
And courage never to submit or yield:
And what is else not to be overcome?
That Glory never shall his wrath or might
Extort from me. To bow and sue for grace
With suppliant knee . . .

JOHN MILTON, *PARADISE LOST* (BOOK I, 106–12)

He [Satan] stood upon the waves a Twenty seven fold mighty Demon
Gorgeous & beautiful: . . .

WILLIAM BLAKE, *MILTON* (BOOK THE SECOND)

I

The devil likes to sing. That surprised me. And he's funny. Not always a laugh-out-loud funny, but funny nonetheless, a "I know what you're saying, man" kind of funny. The first time I heard him say "Honest to God," I looked at him in shock. He gave a sly smile, almost self-deprecating, but not quite, and said, "Ooops." Then in that angelic tenor voice (if I'd ever thought the devil might sing I'd have imagined him a low-register bass) he sang, "When a man is honest, he's a liar; but what Satan says, it's sure as fire; true as earth, strong as iron; the devil, man, he's no liar."

He had a million songs like that, but he didn't really have a songwriter's gift. He's more of a cover man. On some of those, he could blow you away, especially on the sad songs. Or Germanic opera—his tenor could make your spine tingle. His favorite was Wagner because of the *Ring* cycle, especially *Siegfried*. The devil loves all things related to the Norse vision of the world: tragic, fatalistic, grim.

I never really figured out when he first started to shadow me. I'd felt a presence for a while, like someone stood looking over my shoulder all the time. Then one day he just appeared—and I wasn't surprised. That was the kicker. It's almost as if, before that day when he stood (sat, really) before me, I knew he was there. Looking back on it, I should have freaked out. But I didn't. Even now it seems that that whole period was too normal, wrongfully normal—how can the devil be shadowing your every step and that seem normal? But that's how it felt.

Our first talk—and the first time I really saw him—came as I had finished *101 Good Things about Labor Day*. I know that because Jill had left me just before I completed the book—if you can call it a book—and one of the first things I talked to the devil about was Jill. When people asked how Jill and I split up, I always answered, "Happened over Labor Day." A private joke.

I'd always wanted to be a serious writer. Friends would laugh and say they'd rather be like me—a rich writer. But what they meant was a rich hack.

I'd spent two years too many pursuing a doctorate in the history of theology. I'd done the course work, pulled through the five killer doctoral examinations, and I'd done all right. But I could never pull off the thesis.

I tried. I even got three chapters finished. But my committee crucified me, so to speak, at the oral examination. At the University of Chicago Divinity School, at least when I was there, the oral came half way through the dissertation to catch any real problems. Apparently my work was problematic. But I kept plugging away for another two years, trying to walk a tightrope for my committee—a rather old-fashioned church historian, a postmodernist (or maybe he was a post-postmodernist; I was never clear on this as I kept my intellectual head firmly buried in the sands of the fourth and fifth centuries), and a feminist theologian. What a committee, with me constantly teetering along on a tightrope, like I was in the middle of a Leon Russell song. What could I have been thinking? I should have known better. And writing on St. Augustine, of all people. God, I was naive!

So, I turned my part-time job into a full-time one: I wrote abstracts for an index to theological periodical literature. I'd grown to love Hyde Park, where the University of Chicago sits, so I stayed, just like so many poor bastards who never finished their PhDs but still loved the idea of being—in an almost mystical sense—an educated person in an educated environment. Or maybe they were just like me—too lazy to move, too ashamed to go back home with nothing to show for seven years of work and tens of thousands of dollars spent.

I met Jill where we worked; she was a librarian by training and a computer specialist by the necessities of employment, meaning that her two courses in computer applications made her the most qualified person in the office to keep the systems up and running. So, through trial and error and too few continuing education events at company cost, she struggled to manage the computer systems we used to put out our product.

We were an odd pair; me from Tennessee, a little town called Harriman, just off I-40. My family, for a couple of generations, worked at the Oak Ridge nuclear facility. I used to hear my grandfathers on both sides of the family joke about what they called the flashlight benefit—that is, they never need to buy flashlights because they all glowed in the dark. The joke lost its punch as one family member after another died of cancer.

Jill came from the Dells area in Wisconsin; her family had made its money catering to tourists. Her mom ran the miniature golf park and her dad ran a fleet of "ducks," those odd amphibious military vehicles that looked like tanks but could navigate through water as well. Great for a quick survey of the scenery.

Besides being "duck" runners, Jill's family was Catholic. Nothing wrong with that, but my family had embraced homespun Methodism for several generations, very revival come-to-Jesus oriented. And even though I thought I had moved beyond that type of parochial religion to something broader (I was studying Augustine, after all), I still couldn't quite swallow the crazy-for-the-saints attitude of her family.

They lived on a hundred acres. I swear, there were more shrines per acre there than any place in Europe during the Middle Ages, that'd be my guess. The substantial money they made went to building little chapels all over their property. Each one was a work of quality, beautifully appointed inside and out, enough room for five or six adults to fit comfortably inside. Each chapel had a kneeler, a place to light candles, and quite good statuettes of the various saints. They had a fortune in shrines.

Jill's mom, after she retired, held nun day on Mondays and Thursdays, when she'd bring out a cohort of sisters from the local convent and they'd do the chapels, praying the rosary, lighting the candles. That tells you how many of those things they had—it took two full days of hard praying to do all of them, and Jill's mom thought it a shame to let such nice chapels go for more than a week without being used.

Which is to say, a boy who grew up thinking that all you needed was a heart strangely warmed, as that Methodist saint John Wesley preached, probably shouldn't count on fitting into that type of religious world.

Jill no longer felt comfortable with her family's take on true salvation either, and so we were not married in the Church; of course, that meant we were not married at all, in the eyes of Jill's parents. I was the son of a bitch who caused their daughter to live in mortal sin, so I never made it too high on the "son-in-law's we're glad to have" list.

Of course, Jill may have been a bit of a lapsed Catholic, but that didn't mean she'd put up with some Protestant parading around in a robe doing her wedding. She was still Catholic enough to think that, if it was going to be a religious service, it should be performed by someone ordained properly; that is, by a bishop who stood within the line of apostolic succession. So, my family got rubbed the wrong way as well, because I was the miracle child, the only one born to a couple who were never supposed to have children. "Are you going to deny your mother the opportunity to see her only child properly, reverently, and respectably married?" My mother did, in fact, talk like that. Few people in Harriman did, but she taught English at the high school, and sometimes her words came out sounding like a textbook.

Jill and I eloped and essentially created a situation where no one, on either side of the family, liked either of us very much, though they still loved us because their religion said they had to, no matter the terrible thing we had done to them. I know this to be the case because they told us.

Everyone should have a happy wedding, but because we carried the expectations of both our families on our shoulders the weight of guilt took the shine off the day a little. We were happy, but maybe not as joyful as we could have been. I tried to ease the tension with a joke. "Why was the boy melon sad?"

Her eyes rolled. "Not a down-home attempt at humor," she muttered.

"Oh, come on," I said. "Why was the boy melon sad?"

She gave in. "Why?" she asked impatiently, expecting not to laugh. That's always bad when you're trying to tell a joke.

"Because his girlfriend said, 'I can't elope.'" I waited for a laugh; I thought, since it was our wedding day, she'd indulge me with a pity laugh at least. Nothing.

I tried too hard. "Get it? Can't elope. Melons. Canteloupe." I gave her a big grin. She returned a blank look.

I moved on with what I considered to be a better joke.

"What did the French chef say to his pretty assistant?" I asked, a bit too expectantly, given her previous reaction.

She simply arched an eyebrow.

"How about a little quiche, baby?"

With puppy dog eyes, I looked toward her, yearning for approval. The silence made me think perhaps she had not gotten the joke.

"Quiche. Kiss. Get it? They sound a little alike."

She sighed and gave me a pity smile.

Seven years later we went our separate ways. Well, she went her separate way. I stayed pretty much where I was.

Of course, that's because where I was meant a nice penthouse apartment overlooking Lake Michigan, just up from the Museum of Science and Industry on Lake Shore Drive. My books had made me a fairly well-to-do person; though I was an enigma in Hyde Park. Grey matter practically boiled out of the heads of all the professors, students, and ex-students associated with the University. I had been part of that world. But now I was a hanger on, and a bad one at that, because of my gift book writing. The intellectuals scorned me; others envied me. I should have moved, but I couldn't. Jill said that was what was wrong—I was stuck, and it didn't have to do just with physical location.

She left, letting me know that emotionally, mentally, artistically (though she said that with a bit of irony, I think), spiritually, and in every other way I was stunted. A scrub tree in the great forest of life. I wanted to be more; she said I was too comfortable to be more. Maybe she was right.

So there I sat, trying to put the final couple of pages together for my book, *101 Good Things about Labor Day*. Six years before, I had a cute idea: *101 Good Things about Christmas*. Even Jill thought it was cute. Though no graduate of the Art Institute of Chicago, my drawing had a wispish quality to it that drew people's attention to it for a few seconds before they moved on. But, turns out, that sort of time span makes for great commercial property. A few seconds is all most folks are willing to give to a drawing.

For fun, saying it'd make us rich, I'd thrown the first book together. Full of sweet little nothings, Christmas confections, for the Christmas consumer. Every page started the same: "One good thing about Christmas is . . ." The sayings were centered on the page, surrounded by a border that illustrated the words. "One good thing about Christmas is, if you decorate the old-fashioned way with popcorn and candy canes, you can eat the decorations." Trees marched around the edges of the page, all done up in little candy canes and strings of popcorn. The book had 101 pages of that kind of stuff, each page devoted to one saying.

There are nine million copies in print now.

So the "101 industry," as I started calling it, began. We did the major holidays—Thanksgiving, Easter, etc. Then we started in on the minor holidays. By the time I hit Labor Day, I thought I'd die from the saccharine sweetness. But there was no way out. My agent and publisher, realizing that the holidays were at an end, had come up with an idea (and a contract) for the next series: the days of the week. After Labor Day, I had to start almost immediately on *101 Good Things about Friday*.

So I sat there at my computer, filing through the "suggestions" people had sent me via my website for *Friday*. After about the fourth "101" book, I told my agent the ideas had flown the coop. At his suggestion, my website invited "Good Thoughts about Good Days." Not only had I become a hack; basically, I had turned into a plagiaristic hack who simply tweaked the least bad of the ideas that came in on my webpage. Of course, that meant I had to sit down and read through the material. Hell might have been hotter, but I was pretty sure it would at least have been more interesting. Maybe that's when I became aware of the devil's presence enough that I could see him. Or hear him, as it were.

I had my receiver tuned in to WFMT, the fine arts station in Chicago and required listening, especially if you were trying to overcome your hillbilly image and fit in with the UC intelligentsia. Turned out to be a lost cause for me, but I ended up actually liking much of what the station had to offer—Celtic music on occasion, symphonic and chamber music, some of the talk shows. But not opera. I *hate* opera. Those sopranos make me feel like I'm taking a beating at the hands of a spear-toting, horned-helmeted Viking woman.

Sunday, of all days. I loved listening to St. Paul Sundays. I had just heard the St. Paul Chamber Orchestra finish up a nice baroque piece. The host announced that Sir Neville Marriner and the St. Martin-in-the-Fields orchestra were next. I loved ol' Neville. So I relaxed in my seat, waiting for some soothing music to carry me away from my troubles.

But then, singing started.

Zwangvolle Plage!
Müh' ohne Zweck!

Two lines were enough for me to realize an opera had started. I grabbed my remote and turned in my chair to switch the receiver to another station. And there he sat, next to my stereo. Singing. The devil himself.

2

"What the hell . . ." I started.

"No need to be rude, my dear Timothy." A smile flashed across his face, "I may call you 'Timothy,' mightn't I?"

"Uh, well, sure," I stumbled over the words.

Somehow, I knew. I knew it was him. Like an appointment you've made but forgotten until the person shows up on your doorstep. Surprised but not surprised. Or better, taken aback before realizing that, yes, he's supposed to be here.

He sat there in a black pinstripe suit, a rich red shirt, and a gray tie. He wore black patent leather shoes. Very sharp. He looked as if he had stepped off the cover of the defunct *George* magazine—a JFK Jr. look-a-like, though his eyebrows were a bit thinner, his nose a little more narrow. Still, those observations came later. All I knew at the moment was that Jr. had come back to life and was sitting in my living room, singing opera. But I knew it wasn't little JFK.

"People always know," the devil said, an avuncular air about him, as if taking the gosh darn naive nephew under his wing to explain a few things about the world. "Who I am, that is. You do know who I am, don't you, my young Timothy?"

"Yes, yes, I think I do know," I replied.

"Who, then?" he playfully asked.

I took a long look at him. He must have noticed that my eyes rested on the top of his forehead. A guffaw escaped him.

"Oh, come on, Timothy," the devil laughed, enjoying himself. "Don't be so cliched." Then the smile slid down into a frown, and he shook his head at me, chastising my lack of sophistication.

Okay, so I was looking for little horns.

"Come on, say it. Look me in the eye and tell me who you think I am."

And I did. I never did it again, not until the end of our time together. But I looked him straight in the eye, long and hard. At first, it was like falling into a deep well, but the further I fell in, the more I realized, in the distance, fires burned; not like bonfires, but like suns ablaze.

And then I was out. I mostly avoided looking too long into his eyes after that, except for once.

"You're the devil," I finally said.

A sigh blew past his lips. "Such a name for one as I," he said. "Though I knew you were going to say that, especially after I saw you looking for horns." He again took on his avuncular air. "You did study Augustine, didn't you, Timothy? And yet, still so literal minded."

"What would you like to be called?" I asked.

"Lucifer," the devil pronounced. "Call me Lucifer."

I tried to do as he asked, but in my mind I always thought of him as the devil, pure and simple. And, what the heck, that's how he sometimes referred to himself, his early protests to the contrary.

I tried to one-up him with what little I knew of biblical scholarship. "Lucifer's a misnomer, you know," I started, taking on my most authoritative voice. "Isaiah 14:12 refers to a Babylonian king, not to the devil. 'Lucifer' comes from Saint Jerome's translation of the Bible, the Vulgate, and literally refers to Venus, the 'day star.' The term itself has been dropped in most English translations of the Bible since the King James Version. And . . ."

Zwangvolle Plage!
Müh' ohne Zweck!

The devil could be like that sometimes, just interrupt you when you're talking. And usually by singing; very loudly.

I stopped parading my scant bit of scholarship and started listening again.

"Good," the devil said. "Do you have any idea how pedantic you sound when you try to explain things? And it runs through all your writing, except for gift books, which is practically like not writing at all." This time the sly smile that slithered across his face had an edge to it.

"Jerome had it right, at least in his heart, seeing the hidden metaphor, the secret meaning," the devil explained. "Man, I remember those days. Going round and round with him about how to translate this word, how to translate that word. And I even remember . . ."

"Wait a minute," it was my turn to butt in. "You're telling me you knew St. Jerome?"

"Knew him? Loved the guy!" the devil declared. "Now Jerome, he had an air about him, a no-nonsense approach that I appreciate. A hard man, he could be, in the service of his god.

"Yes, he did right; 'day star' for me. The voice of light, the soul of fire. Forget your small-time exegetes; keep with the greats, kid, and learn from them. They're the ones who go for insight, for truth; scholarship, that's for weenies who are too afraid to look reality in the face. I am Lucifer."

He seemed proud to say the word.

"*You* helped translate the Vulgate?" I asked, incredulity punching the words. Jerome had translated the Bible into Latin, and it stood, unchallenged, as the Western church's Bible for over a thousand years. It was the basis for all medieval and Renaissance religious art.

"Why surprised?" the devil asked. "I've known most of the great theologians. Helped them, best I could. Strengthened them. Toughened their minds. Theology's no child's game, you know."

He gave me a sideways look. Then he continued.

"Truth, hard truth, that's where I help. I'll give you an example," he said, putting his fingers to his lips, pursing them as if in deep thought.

"You know Michelangelo's Moses, hillbilly boy?"

"Of course," I said, irritation bubbling up inside me. I didn't like being reminded of my roots, especially when someone used so-called high culture to try to catch me off guard.

"It's a statue," I said, "of Moses seated with the Ten Commandments he's brought down from Mt. Sinai. In the Bible, it says Moses came down from the mountain, and the skin of his face was radiant. By most accounts," I said, though not wanting to state it as a fact, because I was pretty sure the devil was out to trip me up, "Jerome mistranslated the Hebrew word for 'radiant' as 'horns.' That's why there's horns instead of a halo on the statue."

The devil squealed with delight. "Delicious, isn't it? We wrestled with that one for days. But finally Jerome came around. A man who brings commandments from God? What a trip!" His eyes brightened, experiencing the thrill of some victory had long ago.

"Don't you see?" the devil asked. "A man who speaks for God, holding God's commands in his hands. That's something that makes for power! Moses had a tool, and he used it. Yes sir, Jerome finally *got* it. At the heart of every man is a desire for power, and when that power comes, even in the guise of a god's gift—or especially when it comes in the guise of a god's gift—it turns that man into a force. A force to bend men's wills; a force to impose order. Darkness creeps into the heart, and little by little, the light goes out."

The devil exulted in his conquest. "With my help, Jerome finally saw through to reality. Fundamentally, any being who obtains the tools of real power becomes a god unto himself. Jerome knew: coming off that mountain, Moses reflected, more than anything else, everything I stand for."

He laughed to himself. "No, the critics be damned. Jerome knew *exactly* what he was doing when he wrote down that Moses came off the mountain with horns. He finally got the story!"

I simply fluttered my hands in the air, as if to shoo away everything the devil had said. Yet, as I got to know him, I realized that, in some way, he did know the great doctors of theology; I just wasn't sure how much he had contributed to their work. According to him, quite a bit: order, rules, principles, the sort of things that make for an unbending syllogism that, once you're locked into it, you can't fight your way out.

"But you'll find out more about me as we get to know one another," the devil continued. "Let's talk about you. A rich, fairly good looking if a little pudgy, considerate fellow like you sitting here all alone. Pretty bright, if not brilliant. You want more; you don't have it. A self-described *hack*."

Then the devil came closer, laying a hand on my shoulder.

"It's not just a word that describes what you do, my dear Timothy," he explained. "It's who you are. Bit by bit, tedious gift book after another, you're hacking away at your essence. Pretty soon, there won't be anything left."

Then that tenor voice started up again, the third time.

Zwangvolle Plage!
Müh' ohne Zweck!

A flash of light (the devil is such a show-off at times), and the devil stood before me in a doctoral gown, hood and cap included. A blackboard had appeared beside him, and the words of his song had been written there.

"Timothy," he said, in a voice that eerily matched that of my dissertation advisor. "Translate, please." He rapped the board hard with an old-time wooden pointer.

"Er . . . " I started.

"F!" he cried. "Timothy," he said, his voice heavy with disappointment, "how can you have read the great Germanic literature on Augustine? This is easy stuff, and you hesitate?"

He had caught me there. Though my Latin finally, after years, had become passable, I never really learned German. I had to take the German exam three times before passing it. Everyone in the divinity school had to pass French and German. The third try constituted a miracle; I have no clue how I passed.

"Timothy," he said in a sing-song voice, "I know your secret."

I immediately turned red.

"Shame, shame, shame, shame on you!" he sang, a disco beat in the background.

"Too much to do, not enough time to learn," I said, grabbing the first excuse that came to mind.

I knew he knew. I had to pepper my aborted dissertation with occasional notes to the German scholarship on Augustine. I tried my best to find English translations of the German and then painstakingly look up each word in a German-English dictionary to make sure I wasn't making any huge mistakes. Then I'd paraphrase, occasionally making the translation so clumsy that my committee could draw no other conclusion but that I had translated the lines myself. Those few books and articles they drew my attention to that had not been translated into English I paid a PhD candidate in the German department to translate for me. Thankfully, not much of that, or it would have broken my very small piggy bank.

I sighed. "A few words, a phrase here and there, an idiom that got stuck in my head for some reason," I admitted, "that's all the German I know."

"No wonder you don't like opera, then," the devil said. "You don't get it. Of course, Italian would be nice, but, by and large, give me Germanic opera, Wagnerian opera, that's a vision of the world for you!"

He used his pointer, this time more delicately pointing to the words he had written on the board and translating:

Wearisome torment!
Aimless effort!

So we sat there while the devil gave me a mini-lecture on Wagner's *Ring* tetralogy. I knew of Wagner's *Ring of the Nibelungs*, and I even had a slight notion of what it was about. But I didn't really know the details.

So he talked, I listened. He actually made it interesting; more than that, the verses he kept singing at me made sense, both in the context of the opera and in the framework of my life.

The words, turns out, open the third drama of the tetralogy, *Siegfried*. Mime, a dwarf, is singing, slaving away at a sword he is forging, knowing all along that the sword will do no good. Yet, Siegfried requires it, so Mime makes it. But against the great dragon Fafnir, it will fail. And Mime knows it. What a useless waste of time and talent, creating, making, forging an instrument that you know will break when called upon.

How like my life, I thought, and the devil was kind enough to point it out as well. Wearisome torment! Aimless effort! Indeed. God, I hated writing those stupid gift books. I knew more was in me, but what exactly that more was, I didn't know. But I did know that the day had come when sitting down at the computer to work felt like entering the first level of hell. I remember reading Kierkegaard, and he said that despair made every waking moment seem like three o'clock in the morning—that time when you want to sleep, but can't. Every minute, every second, passing in slow motion, time running like molasses, daybreak an eternity away. Wearisome torment, that was it. I guess opera was good for something, if just to help me see the true state of my life.

And talk about aimless effort. I always hoped that, even if the books themselves were so much rubbish, maybe I could do something good, something noble, with the money that came from them. But I hadn't. Didn't even really invest it, like a billion people had advised me to do—while offering to do it for me, for a fee. Millions, just sitting in a bank, drawing minimal interest. Like me, Jill had said. Just like me.

Well, after those fights we had about how we might spend the money, the desire just slipped out of me, like a teenager out his bedroom window, the parents still sitting cheerily in front of the TV thinking all is well.

I'd woven no web of meaning with my hackneyed gains. And so that's why the devil and I talked about Jill, how she'd left. After all, the brutal things she had said about my stunted growth came after a huge fight about money—about me not wanting to give her parents any, about me at least thinking about giving my parents a bit. I should have never played favorites like that, even though at the time I didn't think I was. I really didn't try to see it from her point of view. Maybe that was the trouble—not only didn't I try to see anything from her point of view, I discovered that, by and large, I lived a blinded existence, with no real, committed point of view of my own.

The devil promised to help me fix that, and if I worked at it, he said, I'd discover within myself a true writer. But more of that later. First, Jill.

3

We sat and talked. Believe it or not, the devil is very easy to talk to. When he wanted something out of you, he never interrupted much, just the occasional "I see" to grease along the flow of memories. As I began to open up, he immediately grew a little goatee that he could stroke as I talked, muttering "Ah ha" every now and then. I knew he was dying for me to say he looked just like Sigmund Freud, but I didn't. Already I recognized his angle—he'd take credit for creating psychoanalysis. He stood behind every big event, every creative genius, if you believed him. Sometimes I did. Like falling into a river, going with the flow—easier than swimming upstream.

Well, about Jill. My little Christmas book made a bundle. As far as Jill's parents were concerned, I went from being the bastard who kept their little girl from being married in the Church to the bastard who kept their little girl from being married in the Church who was better off than them now.

So, as you see, things didn't really change all that much.

Still, they knew I'd been at the divinity school at Chicago, studying theology (at least he had the good sense to study a Catholic, I once heard Jill's dad say to her). I had thoughts of being a minister at one time, but I could never really see myself doing the sorts of things a pastor has to do. Jill had filled them in on this aborted bit of career-day mulling, so her parents had decided that, in whatever bizarre or cultish way, I was supposed to be somehow religious.

Jill's mother shook with excitement as she laid out her plan for some of my money.

Shrineland. They wanted to create Shrineland. She rushed through a prepared speech. There would be rides for the kids (The Jordan River Canoe Ride, The Temple Maze, Lazarus's Cave, the Wise Men's Camel Ride, and Jonah's Big Whale Ride represented the Bible rides; the saints would have rides such as St. Francis's Bird of Prey, which isn't how I remember St. Francis thinking about birds; the haunted house would be called Purgatory Pit; two open-air pavilions for the adults—one devoted to music and drink (Gregory's Chants and Chardonnays) and one for religious drama (think Obergammerau and the passion play; only instead of mountains think of mosquitoes big as mountains coming after you—we're talking Wisconsin, after all).

But, of course, the big attraction would be the shrines.

Covered moving sidewalks, that's what Jill's folks had in mind. That way, rain or shine, the shrine route could be run even during inclement weather. We're talking miles of covered walks.

Apparently, Jill's parents overestimated what even a best-selling author makes.

But it wasn't just the money. It's the fact that, well, it was a stupid idea.

I've noticed that, even if parents are held in scorn by sons and daughters, they're still off limits for everyone else. Jill had said often enough that her parents were crazy, bonkers, off the deep end. And I didn't even say that Jill's parents were stupid; just that their idea was.

Jill took it for the same thing.

And I made sure she was the one to tell them "no."

I wasn't making things easy on myself.

But we were at least in the process of mending fences somewhat when, out of the blue, my parents showed up. And they had their pastor with them.

Gyms for Jesus. That's why my parents were there, pastor in tow. To pitch Gyms for Jesus.

Of course, it would start at my parents' church. A big gym would be built; Christian virtues would be taught alongside basketball skills—jump shots for Jesus, free-throw line of grace (where, yes, the shot is free, but you have to put some of your own effort into it—after all, it was a Methodist church we're talking about), slam dunk the devil (the devil actually barked a laugh at that one), passing parables, etc. You get the idea.

From the home gym, there would be "missionary" gyms. They would start in Appalachia, but the pastor had big ideas. Even northerners, he decided, could be saved through Gyms for Jesus. Even in Chicago. Put a nice gym in the slums, bam! A whole load of saved welfare kids, ready to jump off the free-lunch wagon and become productive Christian citizens. My parents and their pastor saw this as, possibly, the only thing to save America, morally and financially, it turned out.

When I didn't say "no" right away, Jill took it to mean that, rather than "our" money, it was really "my" money to do with as I pleased. I did say "no," finally. When I did, my mother pulled me aside and asked, a stage whisper if I ever heard one, "Is it her, dear? Do we need to keep this our little secret?" Of course, Jill heard. Not throwing my mother from the balcony of the apartment at that point constituted treason, as far as Jill was concerned. For days, all she would say was, "So, blood really is thicker than water. Should've known."

But as I talked, and let all the steam out of my pent-up anger toward Jill, I began to listen to myself. I made it sound as if everything were fine until she went wacky crazy over these parental schemes. It just brought a few things to the surface, I suppose. Things Jill and I should have talked about but didn't. A day of wonderful sex followed by a day of silence; a hand-holding afternoon followed by an evening of shouting.

The session, truthfully, helped me. Then the devil had to ruin it a bit, make a little fun, cast his ironic tone over the whole conversation. I got to the end, talking about how, at first, we'd believed love would get us through everything—having no money, parents mad at us, very different backgrounds ethnically and religiously. And such different personalities. Jill was a go-getter; I wasn't. I think that's what she meant when she got angry that last time and said I was stunted.

Still, I thought we could work through it (or, actually, I thought we could just slide through it; Jill pushed for the work part and I never picked up on it). It'd just take love. And that's what I told the devil. Seems funny now, thinking I'd made this final pitch at the end of a sad-sack separation story for love, and to the devil no less! Well, I was green; I'd never spent any real time talking to the devil, so I just blurted out this appeal for love.

Love, I told the devil. We just needed to love more.

I'd had my eyes closed; after a while I didn't want to deal with looking at the devil's Sigmund Freud face. Love, I'd said.

Then I heard that tenor voice, riffing on a 70s love song.

At the tune, my eyes shot open. The devil sat behind a white baby grand, lyrics rolling out of his mouth with a lilting melody, for all the world sounding like Karen Carpenter, crooning on about the world needing "love, sweet love." And as he sang, the devil morphed into Karen Carpenter (which means he wasn't being careful; Richard, her brother, was the piano player, not Karen). My face turned red, him making fun of my confession, especially after I had said I still loved Jill. And as he sang, Karen got thinner and thinner, leaving only a skeleton. Poor Karen; musical sweetheart of the seventies, ravaged by anorexia. A sad end for a girl with such a sunshiny smile.

"Love *and* food," the devil declared after he finished his performance. "The world needs both."

"That's pretty cruel," I said, again not giving much thought (it was the first day, all right?) to whom I was speaking.

"Cruel?" the devil said, hurt peeking around the edges of his voice. "Cruel?"

He stood up. With a whisk of his hand the piano disappeared. By the time he came over to where I sat, he was JFK Jr. again.

"Cruel?" he asked, left eyebrow arching up like a third-rate actor's. "Let me tell you what's cruel," he said. "It's cruel to let the notion get out that love takes care of everything. Maybe love's great, I don't know. But what I do know is this. Without food, you DO die. And there seems to be a whole lotta love in the world for there to be so many starving people."

"Well, sure, but . . ." I began.

"But what?" the devil asked. "There is no 'but' that makes it okay for mommas to watch their babies die of hunger. And not just physical hunger. Poor Karen, I think she had some love, but she was missing something. Some food of some kind. And she starved, inside and out, because, baby, love *ain't* enough."

"Love," the devil went on. "About as useless an idea as you can have."

He threw himself down into the chair next to me.

"I loved Jill," I persisted. "I do love Jill. Now."

"And that's just great, sonny boy," the devil said, casting a tragic look my way. "But don't you know by now? It makes no difference in the way the world runs. That's the big lie. A great feeling, everyone agrees." Then his eyes narrowed as he leaned over toward me, bringing me into his orbit, his sphere, his confidence. With a tone of a fellow conspirator, voice low, he asked, "But it don't really pay the bills, now does it?" Then he winked and said, "And make no mistake. Whether it's the gas company, or the tax man, or God, or the devil, or you and Jill, or you and anybody else, even those who say they love you the most, your own flesh-and-blood parents, it all finally comes down to paying the piper."

That's all he said. But suddenly a wave of images splashed across my mind, the strongest being my parents, sitting there, wanting something from me. Gyms for Jesus. That was the bill. I'd been fed, clothed, sheltered; I'd taken their time, their money, their love. And the bill had come due, and I hadn't paid up. And because I wouldn't put out the cash, the bill had been paid out of the stock of love and affection they had for me. I knew it as soon as I saw the look on their faces. The bank account of affection had been overdrawn to pay what I owed. I'd still be their son; they'd send cards at Christmas; they'd call now and again because they'd see it as their duty. But the relationship had fundamentally changed when I skipped town on the debt.

I'd never thought of my relationship with my parents in that way. And then the images of Jill came.

"You see?" the devil continued, as if on cue. How could he have known what I had seen, or experienced?

"Did you do that?" I asked.

"Do what?" he smiled back at me.

"Put all that in my head, all the . . . stuff I just saw."

"Timothy," the devil said, reaching over and putting his hand on mine. "I am here to teach. You want more. I'll help you be more. But it means seeing life the way it really is. Did I put those things in your head? No. Did I open the door a little so that you could see what's already there? Yes."

I bowed my head, as if ashamed, as if the weight of the world's failure were on my head. "It's not enough, is it?" I asked weakly.

"Love? No, it's not. Not the way this world's set up." Then he muttered under his breath, "Wonder whose fault that is?"

I called out Jill's name, and I cried. But when I looked up, no one was there.

So I got up and went over to my desk. Floodgates had opened within me. No, that's not right. That makes it sound as if the waters continued, the waves washing over me as they had when the devil had opened my mind to the complexities, the frailties, and the ledger-balance nature of human love along with its inabilities, its failures, its broken promises. No, at the computer keyboard it was different. I *had* felt all that; experienced it. But sitting before my computer, I was transformed. The devil had been gone just a few minutes, but the experience felt an eternity away. And now. The experiences opened up to me, the images that cascaded from my mind, pulling, yanking, tugging every emotional rope in my psyche, had now become simply data.

I stood in a vast cavern, frozen, the floods of memory now icy monuments, hard as stone. And I began to examine them, know them. I caressed the cold outlines of everything I had seen. Yes, I thought, this is it. To see, to have the experience is one thing. But to examine it, that's another.

To recognize the experience of love, I saw, was a first step; to be carried away by the sudden recognition of its costs, another; but to be able to describe it in its deliciously detailed intricacy, that was the writer's gift, or so I thought.

And so I wrote. Not a story, not a novel, but scenes. I knew this to be practice, to get good at writing these telling scenes, these rip-the-veil-from-the-reader's-eyes scenes that would uncover the nature of human existence. And building on these scenes of frozen emotion, I would build a fortress of solitude, and my insights would result in *The Great American Novel.*

I was on a tear; I wrote a hundred scenes; then I deleted them all. Real practice, not pretend. And then I slept satisfied, but not without dreams. A dwarf in a cave came to me, and over and over he sang, a beautiful tenor voice I was sure I knew but couldn't quite place:

Das ist nun der Liebe
schlimmer Lohn!
Das der Sorgen
schmählicher Sold!

In my dream, of a sudden, I knew myself not to be in a cave, but in an audience, watching an opera on stage. I turned to the man to my right, starting to ask what the song meant. It was too dark to see him, but his warm breath fell on my ear as he repeated the song, but with words in English:

Now that's awful compensation for love!
That's disgraceful reward for my care!

And as I looked back up on stage, the dwarf and cave were gone, and it was only Jill and me in our apartment, bickering. Then it switched to my home, as a child; then to Jill's. Homely love, made nothing but homely by the perspective of song.

4

Frantic days of writing—just for practice, so every computer bit and byte was trashed at night—brought on odd dreams at night. After a week, I began to wind down a little, and for the first time since the devil's visit I thought I might need to leave the apartment for a while. Maybe a nice dinner out. My stomach growled. I couldn't even remember the last time I ate.

I went through the motions of getting ready for a night on the town; again, I couldn't really remember the last time I had taken a shower, brushed my teeth, or shaved. I had some stubble, but I have a pretty meager beard that's a bit shy of the daylight, so I can go a fairly long time without shaving and not look too bad. It had been a couple of days since the last shave; had it really been the full week? I didn't know.

I dressed casually. Orly's down the street had a nice quiche, with layers of different cheeses baked into it. A really good quiche, it was. I liked it.

Just as I reached for the doorknob on my way out, the doorbell rang. A bit perturbed, because I was really hungry and the prospect of being slowed down didn't sit well, I opened the door and issued a somewhat less than polite, "Yes?"

Standing there in khakis and a blue polo shirt, the devil flashed a grin. "Finally hit the wall, eh? Probably famished."

"Pretty hungry," I replied, opening the door for him to come in. But he stayed put.

"Let's go, then," he said. "Nothing better than good food and conversation." Basically, he invited himself to dinner.

I guess I must have been craving companionship, so I stepped out the door, closed it behind me, and off we went.

I couldn't have had a finer companion. Small chit-chat all the way to the restaurant wove an aura of intimacy between us. He occasionally would place his hand familiarly on my shoulder as he leaned toward me to give emphasis to some little one-liner, usually of quite ironic import. By the time we reached the restaurant, we seemed fast friends.

It wasn't crowded, and a little sign declared "Seat yourself." We headed off for a little table in the corner, away from the few people who sat around nibbling greens or enjoying some after-dinner coffee. We pulled menus from the little stand on the table, though I already knew I wanted the quiche. The devil quickly eyed the offerings, then sheepishly looked at me.

"Not to be forward, dear Timothy," he stated, "but you do realize I don't really carry cash or have a credit card."

If I had been as suave as the devil himself, I would have responded about two seconds sooner and without the initial "er, ah," before getting around to saying, "No worry. I'll take care of it." Then, trying to cover up my lack of smoothness, I winked at him and said, "I owe you, anyway."

"Indeed?" the devil asked, a look of surprise (though fake, I realize now) on his face. "How so?"

I placed my menu down in front of me and leaned forward, a conspiratorial tone of voice, a loud whisper, issued from my lips. "I've been writing," I said.

"Oh ho!" the devil replied, a careful elation spreading across his demeanor like paint being spread over a wall with a roller. "Tell me!" he demanded, as if he simply had to know all the details.

"So many images, feelings, insights," I said, on the verge of a breathiness that, from a woman, might sound a little like seduction. And there was a carnalness, a sensualness, to my newfound ability to wrap my mind around the frozen shapes in my mind and convey those things to paper. An act of creation, in the fleshiest sense possible. So new to me; so powerful.

"They hang there, in my head, and I try out different words for them, poking, prodding, sensing what's right, what's wrong, what works!" Even thinking about it, my whole body trembled, as if I verged on verbal orgasm.

"Easy, isn't it," the devil said, a look of understanding and confidence reaching out to envelop me, "when you really see things for the first time."

But before I could continue, I realized a waiter stood by the table, head cocked, examining me as if I were some exotic creature, a cockatoo in a cage perhaps. With some reserve, he asked, "Are you ready to order?"

Quickly, shyly, quietly, because he knew I was paying, the devil said to me, "Just a caesar salad, please, and a glass of water."

I nodded my head and looked up at the waiter. "The quiche lorraine for me. Iced tea. And a caesar salad and a glass of water for my friend." I gave a half-smile to the waiter, letting him know the order was complete.

"Ah," the waiter said. "Salad and water for your friend. But you'll be paying?"

"Well, yes," I said, a bit put off at such a forward question before the meal was even served. But, then, I had ordered for the devil, so I supposed it to be a fair question.

"Yes, for me and my friend," I said.

With what seemed a rude sound, the waiter stormed off.

"Bee in his bonnet," the devil said, shaking his head. "People aren't so polite anymore, are they?" he asked me.

"No, maybe not," I half agreed.

"Or maybe 'polite' isn't the word," the devil continued. "There's a lack of decorum, of understanding of place in the world. He's a waiter. We're the customers. See it for what it is, Timothy. Look with your new eye. Don't be pushed around."

I thought on that for a minute. True, the waiter had been rude. And as I thought on the event, it did crystallize for me; the gift the devil had given me to see things in a different way worked whenever I wanted it to, not just at the computer.

"That's right," the devil said, interrupting my thoughts, or so I thought; turns out he was simply continuing them. "The eye of the writer is all-seeing, Timothy. The same detachment that has served you so well at the keyboard can be exercised, must be exercised, anywhere, everywhere." With self-satisfaction, the devil proclaimed, "You have been given the writer's gift. Use it well."

The writer's gift. It sounded so extraordinary; felt so extraordinary. The devil was right; it made a difference. My grasp of grammar, or even of style, had not changed—but I had, at least a little.

"Do you *see* what happens when the world is not controlled, unorderly?" he asked. "People are taken advantage of—all the time. I got one word for them—and for you mostly, Timothy: fight. Don't go down without a fight. It's unhealthy. You've let people push you around all your life, thinking it's because you're nice, and you don't really care about life's little insults. As if you're above it all. Look inside you, buddy-o. I think you'll find that you're not. Your soul sits atop a mountain of resentments."

The vision came to me; every little hurt, every little insult, every little shove appeared in my mind, captured in a moment in time, frozen for my inspection. I moved to one in particular, and wrapped my mental hands around its icy form—and my soul burned as if it had touched dry ice. I snarled in pain and anger.

"Sir, your meal," the waiter declared, looking down at me as if a madman. "And your 'friend's' salad and water? Shall I place it here?" Sarcasm dripped from his voice; his words stank, hanging in the air like some acrid eruption of a paper mill smoke stack. He contemptuously placed the salad and water in front of the devil and quickly turned on his heel and started to walk away.

I snapped. "Hey!" I yelled, calling attention to myself, the few others in the restaurant jumping a bit in their seats. But I didn't care.

The waiter turned slowly, a look of exasperation on his face. "Yes?" he asked.

"I don't know who the *hell* you think you are," I said, emphasizing hell, just for fun, thinking it a private little joke between the devil and me, "but I'm a paying customer. A regular customer. I will not be treated in this fashion." I felt my face flushing; the red worked its way up my neck to the top of my head. I had never used this tone of voice on a stranger; but I liked it. Rage boiled up within me, and I simply let it go.

"Bring me the manager," I demanded, throwing my napkin onto the table for good measure. The fellow's name was Jerry; six of seven nights he worked this shift, overseeing things. He knew to see me, being a regular customer. And he knew I had money; there had been enough stories on the sales of my little books in the *Trib* and *Sun Times* for me to be on the radar screen, at least, for most of the locals. I tipped very well; I treated large numbers of people, at times.

Jerry appeared out of the kitchen, a puzzled look plastered on his face. He had heard the commotion and came out to investigate.

"A problem?" he asked, looking at me then giving the waiter the once-over.

"Yes," I declared. "This waiter is simply too rude to put up with. Have I ever complained about the service here, or the food, in any way?"

Jerry allowed as how I had never done such a thing.

And then, something came over me. Maybe the images that had popped into my head had been too much, brought back too many bad memories. I blurted out, "Fire him!"

"What?" Jerry asked, not believing what he had just heard.

I took on the best dead-level tone I could muster, despite the fact that I was shaking inside. The rage had hold of me, and I thought my insides would explode. This was new territory for me, but I was determined to explore it as fully as possible.

"Fire him, or I never come back," I demanded. "And I'll tell all my friends never to come again."

I could see Jerry considering it, but I couldn't tell where he'd come down.

"I'll write something," I blurted out, "send it to the papers. Talk about the decline of 'decorum' in restaurants." I stole a glance at the devil, and he gave me a little smile, obviously pleased I had picked up on his observation. Then I delivered the coup de grâce. "And Orly's will be front and center," I declared, "as a prime example of everything that's wrong with restaurants today."

That did it. Jerry was a manager, and a good one. He knew a business decision when he saw it. My stature as an author helped me here; actually, I probably couldn't have broken into the *Trib* except on the obituary page, truth be told. But all Jerry knew was that I was a famous writer (which meant he didn't know enough about the biz to recognize that "rich" didn't necessarily mean "famous," not in the sense of influence or appreciation), and so he turned to the now-wilting waiter and said, "Come in for your check tomorrow. You're fired."

The waiter began to babble a bit. "Leave now," Jerry said, "or I call the cops." Jerry turned to me and said, "I'll get you a new waiter," then turned to go back to the kitchen, without looking to see if the newly unemployed had left yet or not. His posture was clear—he fully expected him to be gone, or he would call the police.

The waiter turned and walked slowly out the door.

Maybe it was the adrenaline rush; I wasn't really hungry anymore.

And so I looked at the devil to see what he was up to—mostly he had moved the salad around on his plate. "Let's beat it," I said to him, getting up without waiting for his agreement, slapping thirty bucks on the table for the bill. A waiter rushed out toward us, but I simply called back over my shoulder, "We're done."

The walk home was quiet. The devil hummed some song or another—maybe one of his operas, but I wasn't sure—while I went over the scene again and again in my head. My stomach knotted up—I realized I was hungry. I'd have to order a pizza because I hadn't eaten very much in several days. A weird feeling. Like what I had done was just right; I shouldn't have had to take that waiter's guff. I was the customer, for crying out loud. And it was like all the times in the past when I had let things slide; but seems they just slid right down into some place in my memory where the scoreboard flashed "zero" for my side, and I was tired of always being so far behind.

But it was wrong, too. Wrong for me. It wasn't like me to yell at someone like that. I was a nice guy; in all the good ways that attribution can be meant, and all the bad ways. People did walk all over me, at least more than they should. But I also think some people's lives were, at least for a little while in some place or another, a little more tolerable because I had been nice to them when I didn't have to be. Why did the wrong sorts have to take advantage of that?

Before I knew it, we were back at the apartment. I called one of the multitude of pizza parlors in Hyde Park that serviced the academic community, which meant a whole lot of penny-pinching grad students who rarely had the money for a really good tip. I sat down to wait. Finally, the devil spoke.

"Write before you forget," he said.

"Write what?" I asked, beginning now to feel a huge let-down after the little scene in the restaurant.

"What you were thinking before," the devil said. "Use this. Don't waste your writer's eye, and don't waste your experience." As if reminding me ever so gently of things Jill had said, he exhorted, "Grow, Timothy, grow. Put this to good use. Remember the images from the restaurant, the ones that spurred you to do something you've never done in your whole Milquetoast life." I started to object, but he simply threw up a hand and, rather gently, said, "Grow."

And so I sat down at the computer. This time, I decided to give my writing more of a story form, complete with a title.

"The Slow Death of Nice People"

My fingers flew. The story opened with a clear-eyed analysis of a recent slight. I had been in McDonald's, waiting forever for service. The line was six deep when I first walked in; after five minutes, it was still five deep. After fifteen minutes, one person still stood in front of me. I watched as every move of the server played as if in a slow-motion movie. I had an appointment, and now I was going to be very close to being late—I *hated* being late. And the entire McDonald's staff acted as if intent on keeping me in their restaurant as long as possible.

Finally, another server came up and keyed in to the register. I started to step over, finally ready to give my order, when someone from behind me, *who had just come in*, sped around me to the register, rattling off his order before he had even taken his last step or two up to the counter.

I used all the pent-up anger I had writing the scene. A coherent story took shape. I barely realized the devil was there. He must have turned on the TV; at some point, I thought he must be watching some soap opera, because I heard about a guy who had just come home from losing his job, and before he could even explain to his wife what had happened and how unfair it had been, she scooped up their baby and left. Sounded like for good. But that's all I caught. Too caught up by the muses.

As I typed the last word, I heard a familiar guitar riff, a sound from my past. I turned and saw the devil, guitar in hand, step up to the mike that now stood in the middle of my living room. Colored spotlights swirled about him as he sang "Taking care of business." His hair had gone all permed, just like ol' Turner used to wear it, and he played through the whole chorus, sounding for the world like Bachman Turner Overdrive coming over the radio.

For a moment, I remembered something from St. Augustine. He believed the devil had no real substance of his own—it was all borrowed, stolen, taken. And, for just a second, that insight flashed into my head, like a revelation. The devil can never really be anything more than an imitator. He's an aper, pure and simple.

But then the devil gave a sweep of his hand and a bow, my moment of insight disappeared like a bad magic trick, and he said, "Good for you, Timothy, good for you." The devil had effectively and quickly pulled my attention back to myself. "Put it down, these feelings, the *reality* of these feelings. It's a start. Keep working at it.

You've practiced long enough. Make a good short story out of this. From the way it sounded, you've already got the first draft."

I nodded my head. My earlier suspicions about the devil flew from my head as I thought about my story, where it would end up. The insides of the protagonist would suffer death because of all the small insults of the world, and he'd snap, in some explosive, outrageous way. Maybe at a restaurant, because just one snotty waiter too many looked down at him, ignored him, took advantage of him, and then finally killed off the last remnant of niceness left in him. And then the guns would blaze.

I had a story here. I tipped my head toward the devil, acknowledging his hand in my transformation. Or, at least, the transformation I thought was taking place—me becoming a real writer. I came to understand later something else entirely was going on.

5

Old habits die hard. Maybe that's why Aristotle pushed "habitus" so much in his ethics. Routinize good behavior enough, and it continues mindlessly on. I guess that's how I found myself in church the next Sunday. If I had stopped to think for half a second, I might have seen the irony of someone in league with the devil heading off for Sunday service, but I didn't stop to think: I just went.

Much like my life. After that initial frenzy of practice writing, input and delete, input and delete, I had finally started the real thing. Writing. I worked as a writer. The feeling washed over me the minute I hit "save" on the computer screen, committing the scenes I had written for "The Slow Death of Nice People" to the banks of memory that magically remembered every finger stroke I made. No, I no longer rampaged through days and nights preparing myself to be a writer, exercising my writer's eye. I was writing a short story, and it was coming along splendidly.

And my normal life had resumed, complete with bathing and eating on a regular schedule.

Church was part of my regular life, so off I went, happy to be on my way, unaware that hypocrisy nipped at my heels as I walked briskly along the street.

I made my way up to St. Augustine's Episcopal Church. I liked the name, but not for the obvious reason: the Episcopal St.

Augustine was a far different character than the St. Augustine I had wrestled with for years as a subject of study and finally of the aborted dissertation. *The* St. Augustine was a bishop in Hippo, North Africa, and he almost single-handedly crafted the language and method that would dominate Western theology for centuries, indeed, for well over a millennium.

The *other* St. Augustine held a certain appeal for me, just because he and I may have had more of a family resemblance, so to speak, than I had with the great doctor of Hippo. The Anglican church's St. Augustine (the Episcopal church in the U.S. is a daughter church of the Anglican Communion) was, politely put, a bit timid. One of the truly great popes and one who deserved the appellation, Gregory the Great, had sent the good Augustine off to convert the barbarous peoples of Britain. The Irish had already started making good headway coming in from the north of the island, and Gregory knew Rome needed a foothold if the place wasn't to be held permanently under the sway of St. Patrick.

Augustine was less than thrilled.

Gregory packed him off in 596. By the year 597, Augustine still loitered about northern Gaul (one day to become France), in no hurry to fulfill his mission. He had heard stories about the big island; the tales that swam across the channel did not inspire the good saint-to-be with missionary zeal. By some accounts, he was scared witless.

Finally, Gregory ran out of patience, and Augustine reluctantly went, settling down eventually in a place called Canterbury after winning the King of Kent to the ancient faith. Thus, Augustine helped establish the See of Peter's power in yet another land. It took another hundred and fifty years or so, but followers of Patrick finally lost out to Rome, being as the kings of many kingdoms within what was slowly on its way to becoming England decided that, all other things being even, they'd just as soon be on the side of the guy holding the keys to heaven. Peter and the pope made for quite a pair, and so the tradition of Patrick ended up mostly contained on the smaller island of Ireland, from whence the tradition came.

So how's that? A guy with little zeal and even less courage ends up getting to be the patron saint for a place like England. You got to like a fellow like that, who just kind of fell into being someone history remembered as a "founder." Holds out hope for people like me.

Well, of course, it wasn't just that. After all, I had been raised Methodist—renegades running out on the Church of England even after our good founder, John Wesley, said not to. And Jill was Catholic; and to some degree the Anglicans still maintained some semblance (even the pope said so) of apostolic tradition. So the Episcopal Church seemed like a natural for us—I'd step up a bit, liturgically speaking, Jill would step down a smidgen, and it made for a nice compromise. Catholic-lite, that's what it was. Enough different from the Church of Rome to hold at bay the Protestant in me; enough like "The One True Holy Catholic and Apostolic Church" (as Jill referred to it) to satisfy her.

Plus, the academic/scholar/literary type in me appreciated both the grounding in history and the language of the Prayer Book. Win-win all around.

I had never bumped into Jill at church since she left me. I think she may have been visiting a Catholic church, trying it on again, like pulling out some old piece of clothing to see if it still fit (I thought of a cheerleader uniform for a minute then remembered I was in church).

I took my seat, and soon the processional hymn started. It was one of my favorites. The organist played an intro, then the congregation burst into song.

As longs the deer for cooling streams
in parched and barren ways,
so longs my soul, O God for thee
and thy refreshing grace.

My voice is quite decent, and, for some reason, my spirit soared. So I filled my lungs and let loose. But as we sang along, a beautiful tenor descant soared along on high notes during the fourth stanza.

To Father, Son, and Holy Ghost,
the God whom we adore,
be glory, as it was, is now,
and shall be ever more.

Haunting, it was; beautiful, but not, for some reason, matching the congregation's voice. A little out of place. Too loud? Too soft? I'm sure it was pitch perfect on note. But something was . . . wrong.

And then I knew.

I scanned the congregation as the priest began, "The Lord be with you." The response came automatically to my lips, "And also with you." And then I spotted him! The devil sat up near the front, gleaming in a white suit. He turned his head and flashed a smile at me, and then he was gone.

I tried to see where he had run off to, when someone stepped from the side aisle and moved next to me. I glanced over and saw the devil, grinning as if he were in a contest with the Cheshire cat. I wondered if he would disappear and leave that enormous set of dazzling white teeth behind.

After the Summary of the Law and the Collect for the Day, we sat. A bit confused, I squirmed in my seat. Finally, the devil leaned over and said, "Relax, dear Timothy. I'm here to help." He placed his hand on my knee and gave it a good-natured pat. "Besides," he continued, "I like church. Good music much of the time."

I sat there wandering what he meant by "help." I soon found out.

As a reader droned through a very long Old Testament lesson, trying his utmost to keep any semblance of tonal variation out of his voice, the devil said, "Let's find out what church is really about."

I raised my eyebrow, an unspoken question. I didn't want to speak during the Scripture reading.

"Thoughts, Timothy. I'll let you in on some of the thoughts I hear during worship." And then that familiar hand rested momentarily upon the back of my head. And when I looked over again, he was gone.

We moved to the psalm. It occupied me for a moment, reading responsively from Psalm 137. A swell psalm that starts of well enough—a phrase so recognizable that it had been used for everything from a book title to a play title to, of all things, a Don McLean song, sharing vinyl space with "American Pie." And so the reader said, "By the waters of Babylon, there we sat down and wept, when we remembered Zion." By the next verse, my mind had moved to the cool Godspell song, "On the Willows There," which came from the next verse. By all accounts, a great start to a psalm; very moving, very inspirational.

But then we had to get to the end—less familiar ground. The psalm ends up talking about dashing the heads of the enemies' children against the rocks.

And then the surprise began.

I looked up at the monotone master (from the old school, the less feeling the better, makes it seem serious and religious), and I stared at him for a moment as we finished up the gory part of the psalm. Then I heard him, clear as day, with all kinds of emotion in his voice, saying, "That's disgusting." But as I looked at him, his lips had not moved.

I continued to watch him, concentrate on him, as he moved away from the lectern, crossing the path of the Epistle reader, both genuflecting before the overly dressed Jesus on the cross. "Damn," I heard the voice say, "I've got to talk with Father Reece about this genuflecting crap. My knees can't take it anymore."

I closed my eyes, and the sound stopped.

I turned my attention toward Father Reese. As if sitting next to me, speaking right into my ear, I heard him say, "I've got to find a better sermon service. Maybe I can learn how to surf the Internet and find sermons, or at least ideas. I should be embarrassed to repeat the pablum those fools in St. Louis count as a sermon."

And I found that, by concentrating a little harder, I could get at the thoughts that underlay the surface thoughts. I could see Father Reece's trembling hand, as if it were my own, writing out a check to "Sunday Sermons," and he placed the check in a pre-addressed envelope with a destination of St. Louis, Missouri.

Astonishment hit me, for some reason. I would have never guessed that Father Reese used one of those sermon services. He had a PhD, for crying out loud, one of the reasons he was serving a church in super-cerebral Hyde Park.

I spent the service reading people's thoughts. Turns out, very few were focused on the good Father's canned sermon. I don't know if that should have been a source of comfort for him or dismay. Maybe they didn't listen because the sermons weren't very challenging. Or maybe they didn't need to be challenging because no one was really listening—so why waste the effort of worrying through proper exegesis and rhetorical strategies.

I got enough thoughts to fill a book—or a least a good short story. An idea began to take shape in my mind. We hit the part of the liturgy where we sang the Agnus Dei—O Lamb of God, who takes away the sins of the world, have mercy upon us. The delicious irony of it all. All these on-the-surface pious souls, for all the world looking like little angels in church, while the whole time it turns out the blood of the lamb might be the only thing that could wipe away the stains on their hearts. Such a story. It would be like shooting fish in a barrel, it'd be that easy to lampoon the service.

The heart of the story came as Communion took place, though the shock of it kept me from realizing that until later as I actually started writing. And because of what I saw at Communion time, the tone changed from lampoonish to something quite darker.

A pleasant looking teen made her way up to the altar rail, a wisp of a smile sitting demurely on her lips. A pious look, I thought. She's trying to look pious. Like a renaissance painting, a Da Vinci smile. Barely there, hinting at something—more. But what? Real or fictive, that smile? I couldn't tell.

But then I knew. It was a look that she desperately hoped covered up her fears, her insecurities, her loneliness. She thought the little hint of happiness masked her real self.

Her real self. The thoughts that dogged her all the way up the aisle, and as she prepared to receive the body and blood of Christ, were, over and over again, "Nobody likes me. Why don't people like me? I try to be nice, but all they do is make fun of me."

Her clothes showed a little wear—they were nowhere near new. Her hair fell neatly over her shoulders, but there was no sign of a custom cut. And then I saw her shoes.

Again, I knew, looking a little deeper below the surface, that she had bought these new shoes for church. Proud that they had no scuff marks, no visible defects. Last year's fashion, but still nice enough as long as they weren't often worn—too cheap to stand up to much use. Bargain shoes.

Then I realized that everyone who cared to look knew they were bargain shoes—no mind reading necessary for that, just decent eye sight.

She had forgotten to wash the price off the bottom of the shoes. As she knelt at the altar, the bottom of her shoes sticking out for all the world to see, one could read $4.99 written across the tan outer sole in black marker. The dollars and cents of it screamed "bargain bin!"

A heard a titter of laughter. I immediately looked over across the aisle, where a group of self-assured, golden-child teenagers sat. I reeled from the thoughts I read—mean spirited, domineering, intent on humiliating and hurting, while the blood of Christ still lay wet on their lips. Once they left this memorial to mercy, they would be merciless. They would do all they could to kill what spirit the child still had in her. I shuddered.

I couldn't stand it. They would find some way to hurt that poor girl that would stick with her for the rest of her life. And so I left, sick with the thoughts tainted with sin, the malice of minds at worship strangling me.

I slipped past some startled ushers, tripping over my own feet—my shoe laces had become untied—in my hurry to leave. I hit the door hard with one hand on my way down, knocking the bar so the door flew open as I continued to fall. I lay there, half in and half out. A hand appeared, offering to help me up.

I started to say "thanks," but as I looked up, I saw the man's face, and his thoughts came at me megaphone loud. "What a klutz. Makes millions writing stupid doodads and can't spend a dime on shoes that'll stay tied. Heard his wife left him. No wonder."

I yanked back my half-outstretched hand. "No, thanks," I blurted out. I pulled myself up and left, not worried about dignity, just speed.

But I slowed down as I went along. I veered to the east a couple of blocks so that I could walk along Lake Shore Drive. A nice breeze created little whitecaps out on the waves. I calmed down a little. I passed an elderly couple, and I looked hard at both of them. I think they thought I might be a mugger or a pervert or both and gave me a defiant look, but I just smiled and walked on past.

I had heard nothing. Whatever the devil had done to me, it apparently only worked back at the church. I was left with just my own thoughts, and that was enough for the time being.

6

I ended up down by the lake, eyes closed, listening to the waves. Sunday morning in Hyde Park, especially by the lake shore, whispered at you rather than yelled. During the week, and even on Saturdays, the roads are clogged with traffic, and the Museum of Science and Industry does a great business of pulling in every school child within a day's drive. But on Sunday, all that's gone—just a few quiet vehicles on the way to nowhere in particular in no particular hurry. I closed my eyes and relaxed, trying to purge my mind of church, or, as it were, anti-church, like a parallel universe, matter and antimatter reversed or something. Star Trek bizarre, that's what it was.

A soft voice broke through my temporary Nirvana. "Don't forget it, Timothy, use it." I opened my eyes, and the devil stood in front of me, three-quarters turn, so he wasn't really looking straight at me. I realized he resembled every mail-order catalog model I'd ever seen. He stood there in his white suit, one hand in his pocket, a pensive look on his face, hair blowing slightly in the breeze.

Then he sat down next to me. Posing time was over. He gave me a gentle slap across the back of my head, like a big brother joking around. And, in the most sincere voice he ever used with me, he asked, "What'd you expect?"

"Not that," I said simply. I didn't have anything else to add.

"You've read Augustine. Didn't you pay attention? It's all about sin."

The pain ran too deep. I decided to parry the devil's seriousness with a little joking of my own.

"A Methodist born and bred, raised on the pure milk of Wesleyan perfectionism." I gave off a little snort. "What chance did I ever have of really understanding Augustine? Besides, I fell for the early stuff, Augustine's *Confessions*, things like that. Not the super hardcore sin and depravity stuff."

"You got a point there, my boy," the devil replied, ready to let me take the lead, moving into more familiar territory of humor and irony. "You lived your formative years in a place that only recognized little 's' sins—particular sins that, in the best of Methodist worlds, could be swatted down like some pesky mosquito with the fly-swatter of effort aided by grace."

I laughed at his characterization.

"Of course, you know, for Augustine, all those little 's' sins were simply a result of big 'S' Sin, the Condition, the wreck of human nature," the devil continued. "Humanity isn't condemned for what it's done, but for what it *is*."

"I know," I agreed. "Just never really *knew* it, though, if you get my drift." I paused. "Not until today, anyway."

"It's tough, seeing the truth," the devil replied. "Make no mistake: Augustine was one tough guy."

I sat a little while, a melancholy mood enveloping me, not ready for anything serious but still not able to overcome the agony of being in a church service and really knowing what was going on.

"Talking about sin, once knew a minister who almost got fired talking about sin," the devil said.

I turned my head, encouraging him to go on.

"Yeah, he was talking about sin. Doing a good job, too. Made them all squirm in their pews a little bit. And then, just like Augustine, and just like Paul before him, he tried to talk about how the little sins that they mostly laughed at come from a place—an essence, actually—inside that is nothing but sin, a sinful nature. People aren't much for that anymore."

"No, not much," I said.

"No, not even the Presbyterians have hung on to it," the devil agreed. "Piskys have some good language about it in the Prayer Book, as you well know. What's it they say about Episcopalians? Augustinian in their prayer book, Pelagian in their pulpit. So, they pray as if they're completely depraved and in need of God's grace, preach like they're good folk who just need to try a little harder. Pretty much true, don't you think?"

"Yep," I agreed. "Priest uses the sermon mostly to cover over what the Prayer Book says."

"Anyway," the devil said, "this fellow, he was talking about sin. And he used the language I just used. Talking about how lying and cheating and all that stuff is just little 's' sin. But then he moved on to human nature itself, and he started talking on and on about big "S" Sin, the stuff Augustine and Paul hammered away at." The devil chuckled.

"What happened?" I asked, into the story at this point.

"Well," the devil said, a smile licking the corners of his mouth, "the congregation had a lot of older people in it, and most of them thought, when he said big 'S' Sin, that he was saying big "ass" sin. They thought he was being vulgar—a sin for a minister on a payroll if ever there was one. A lot of explaining and apologizing went on so that he could hold onto his job—a perfect example itself, I suppose, of *both* big 'S' Sin and big 'ass' sin." And with that, the devil let loose a whoop.

I started laughing and couldn't stop. Looking back on it, the story really wasn't that funny, but I needed to laugh, because laughter held back the images from church.

After we both settled down a bit and had sat in amiable silence for a couple of minutes, I said, "Surprised to see you at church today."

"Me? I love church," the devil said.

"How come?" I asked.

"Music, for one thing. Whether it's sixteenth-century Anglican—Tallis and I got along fabulously—or good ol' foot-stomping gospel, I like the music."

We both mused on that for a bit, then the devil offered up, "I do like the Episcopal hymnody on this side of the pond. Those folks still look to the Mother Church in England, so they pull in people like Tallis—and Ralphie."

"Ralphie?" I asked.

"You know, one of your favorites—Ralph Vaughan Williams. I always called him 'Ralphie,' just for fun," the devil said. "He hated that name. Good student, though."

I raised an eyebrow, ready for the story.

"Yeah, Ralphie was good. Not as good as when I helped him, but good. Hymn settings, symphonies, studies in folk music, all of it. An adjustment here, a little tweak there."

Deciding to indulge the devil, I asked, "So, what was your favorite piece that you 'helped' with," emphasizing my willingness to listen while also withholding judgment on the devil's real role in Williams's musical development.

"Well, some of the things we collaborated on are simply standards, aren't they?" he asked, though it really wasn't a question, him giving off a knowing air, as if his collaboration, obviously, really made the pieces great. "There's our *Variation on a Theme by Thomas Tallis*. Great deal of fun. And *The Lark Ascending*. You know those pieces, surely?"

I presumed the devil already knew I did—I had been playing both recently when he had come to visit. So I just nodded.

"My favorite? That'd have to be Symphony No. 5." He looked off at the lake, something wistful in his demeanor, as if his mind were skimming over the waters, off to a different place and time.

A few moments passed before he spoke again. "It was *fun*," he emphasized. "Always fun with Ralphie. Became a running joke with him. I'd say, 'Ralphie, where are the English horns? You're English, aren't you? For crying out loud, play the horns, man, play the horns." He winked at me, a familiar touch he sometimes added, his eyeballs rolling upward, practically inviting me to look for devil horns on his head. "I'd always say it, then he'd always shoot back, 'You know good and well that the *cor anglais*'—he always insisted on the fancy French name—'isn't a horn at all. And it isn't even English!' Every chance I got, 'Play the horns, man.'"

"And he did, every now and again. In the Fifth, listen to the third movement. I know you've got the CD. Even Ralphie admitted it fit better than any other instrument for the mood. He admitted it straight up." Then he barked out a laugh, "Not like his studies of English folk songs. I told him, English horn, English horn. The fellow originally wrote them for the cello, if you can believe *that*." He said it as if the idea of the cello was ludicrous, but I have no idea why that would be. He continued, "I got the last laugh when he went back and arranged them for English horn." The smile of a triumph experienced decades earlier lit up his face.

He cleared his throat. "Thinking back on it all, the whole construction of the Fifth, what you have to realize is that the thing that really picks the piece up is the timpani." He turned on the bench so that he faced me directly. "Can't have too much timpani, if you ask me."

He paused to let me comment. I didn't.

"Anyway," he said, "listen to the first and fourth movements. You'll hear where the timpani drives the action. A symphony is like the animal kingdom. Listen, you'll hear it. Especially in Williams's Fifth. When the horns hit in the big crescendos, it's like elephants trumpeting. The strings? They're the gazelles, bounding along the plain. And then there's the timpani. Like a lion. Going to and fro. Pushing the music where it needs to be. The timpani's great. My favorite instrument. It can give off a royal rumble, move to a majestic roar. And always, always, driving the strings like gazelle across the plain. Listen some time. You'll hear it if you try." Then a frown touched his lips. "Of course, it would have resolved better with a grand finish and more timpani at the end. Just kinda whimpers out, if you ask me. I told Ralphie that, but he could be stubborn sometimes."

I shrugged my shoulders. In the range of things the devil had told me, this lesson in music didn't seem terribly important.

The devil sensed my growing disinterest and sighed. "Well, maybe you just don't get how important the timpani is. That's okay. Some things you just may not be constitutionally fit to understand."

"You think I don't understand music?" I asked.

"Oh no," the devil shot back. "You probably understand music okay." Then he slipped the knife in. "But timpani is about, as I said, *drive*. That may be what you don't get. Not yet."

I didn't feel like getting into an argument, so I didn't take the bait. Instead, I decided to change the topic back to the church music we had been discussing before he went incredibly far out of the way, I thought, to insult me.

"What about the words?" I asked. The devil let a question mark hang in the air between us. "You know," I explained, "back in church. The words that go with the music. Like that first hymn, references to the Trinity and all. Doesn't that bother you?"

"Eh," he said, rather nonchalantly, "You learn to tune that out after a while. Focus instead on what one can appreciate, even love. Think about Leonard Bernstein and his treatment of Bach's St. Matthew Passion. He's Jewish; the words, quite obviously, Christian. A broad-minded soul trumpets beauty wherever it is to be found."

I was intrigued by the devil's attitude. I thought, "Wow. What if I could get this down for the record: An Interview with the Devil on Why He Goes to Church." Of course, no one would believe me. So I just kept on talking.

"What else? Just the music? I imagine you like what I heard today in everybody's head. Anything else."

"Communion," the devil replied. "You gotta love Communion."

"Really?" I asked, a bit perplexed. "Why Communion?"

"Well, look at the different ways it can be done," the devil said. "There's Baptist simplicity and Roman ritual. Elegant prayers and heart-felt tears of remembrance. Quite extraordinary, really. It can be aesthetically pleasing, to say the least, whether in high culture or homespun ways."

"I thought you'd like it because it reminded you that you got the best of God, at least for a few days," I declared, perhaps needlessly needling the devil. Maybe not such a good thing to do. But he took it all in good humor.

"Oh no, Timothy, don't think I'm that stupid!" he said, a sophisticated air and a look of the eye to let me know he thought me too engaged in lowbrow thoughts.

"I knew who He was from the beginning. No way. Your kind did that job all by yourselves. Besides," he sniffed, superiority unabashedly coating his words, "that had nothing to do with me. Great battle? Nope. I don't hold your kind in thrall, there was no rescuing to be done, at least not from me. I persuade, not coerce. Those who side with me do so clear eyed and willing."

The conversation had begun to take too serious a turn for my taste at the moment, so I steered us back to Communion.

"Okay, besides the *aesthetics*," saying the word in as pinched and snooty as way as I could, "what else do you like about Communion?"

"Well, it can be great fun, can't it?" he replied. "Do you know how many times the past two thousand years someone has dropped the host or spilled the wine? There's always a loud clanging, and people jump out of their seats, unaccustomed to anything but dirge-like funeral music while taking Communion. Clerics scurry around like rats, trying to pick up the crumbs, lick the juice off the floor. Say holy things to try to cover up human clumsiness. That's religion in a nutshell anyway, isn't it?" he only half-asked, because it really wasn't a question in his mind but a bald statement.

"I suppose," I replied. Small guffaws pulled at my insides. I had nearly forgotten the time when I was a kid and the Communion tray, full of grape juice (I was a Methodist, after all, as was that bastion of Methodist temperance, Mr. Welch, who had grape juice to sell to churches), fell to the floor. So much commotion, you would have thought it an absolute national emergency, the kind that showed up on the eleven o' clock news. Even as a kid, my mind saw the venerable news anchor David Brinkley sitting behind his desk: "This just in. The Communion tray fell to the floor today in a small Methodist church in Tennessee. Though there were no fatalities, grape juice did splatter, ruining several very nice white sweaters. More later as information becomes available."

My sides shook a little. The devil winked at me. "I remember," is all he said.

More time passed. Then, rather thoughtfully, the devil added, "There are other reasons to attend Communion. You learn about what makes people tick, what's important. What they'll die for; what they'll kill for."

"What do you mean?" I asked.

"Well, I remember one time, back, oh, sixteenth century sometime. Protestants had just started causing a ruckus, Catholics were on the defensive, then they were on the offensive. Wars, battles. I remember once, the Catholics won the day. They captured the local Protestant ruler—somewhere in Germany, no, it was called the Holy Roman Empire back then. Anyway, they dragged this fellow off to church, held Mass while having the trussed-up royal watch, then burned his eyes out, so the 'right way' of seeing Communion performed would be the last thing he ever saw. What's funny, the way the Protestants—these Protestants, anyway—were doing Communion was pretty much like the Catholics, except they did it in German instead of Latin. 'In remembrance of me.' Hmpf! Can't imagine He gets much of a kick out of that."

"No," I answered, "I can't imagine so." All of a sudden, I felt tired. "I'm going back home now. You coming?" I asked.

"Oh, I think I'll enjoy the view here for a little while, then there's someplace that I need to be. As special as I think you might turn out to be, Timothy, I do have other folks I need to spend a little time with. New friends like yourself, old friends who need a nudge." He winked at me, once again pulling me into his orbit with a bit of conversation and body language. He did it so easily; I followed without thinking. That seemed to be the way of it, most of the time. Looking back, I wonder how many others had been so easily led along, like a dog on a leash.

"How about dinner tomorrow night?" he asked.

I couldn't remember anything on my calendar. "Okay, sounds great. Meet at my place?"

"I'll be there with bells on," the devil replied, lifting his hand in, what? Dismissal? More that than a good-bye wave, I thought.

So I ambled on home, taking the lift to the penthouse. I walked over to the windows that overlooked the museum and the lake, peering down to see if the devil still sat on the little bench on the shore. No, he was gone.

Though tired, I found that I could not rest. At first, I turned on the TV and started watching a little bit of the Bears game. But the physical violence of football reminded me of the spiritual violence of the church service. I turned the TV off.

I tried to take a nap, but I only ended up tossing and turning.

Finally I wandered over to the computer.

I had never really written on Sundays before. Again, Methodist upbringing, I suppose. The Lord's Day was to be kept holy, and that meant no work. I sighed. Actually, not just a good Christian sentiment. It struck me for the first time how, maybe, it was a class thing as well. The right kind of people didn't *have* to work on Sunday. We marched piously off to church, to give God His due, bow in reverence on the day meant for such, and then, because it was a day of rest, we'd head off to the local diner for Sunday lunch. No, we didn't work on the Lord's Day, but we—and that meant the whole church-load of us, because most of us usually ended up at the diner—certainly saw to it that the folks who cooked for us, waited on us, and cleaned up our mess after we had gone had plenty to do on the day of rest.

Geez, I thought to myself. Have I gone entirely cynical? About everything? I didn't know.

But what I did know was that the images from the morning had begun to settle down. The emotion had begun to wash away. The events had taken on that icy glaze of moments caught in time. And instead of recoiling—or running, as I had literally done that morning—I began to stroke the memories, at first running a mental hand over the smooth surface of pain frozen in time. Then I stepped back and started to analyze, to use my "writer's eye," as the devil called it.

The girl with the mousy-brown hair called to me. I needed to catch each glint of humiliation, capture every despairing look, trace the path of loneliness so worn into the ground of her soul.

I started typing. At first, slowly, as my fingers felt for the expressions that would best convey the hidden horror of church; I wanted hints, glimmers, not fully exposed gore, at least not at first. So I gently, thoughtfully, pecked at the keyboard. No, that's too harsh a word. Not pecked; that's too fast an action word. The slight movement of my fingers resembled nothing so much as a blind man, trying for the first time to run his fingers over Braille, attempting—however haltingly, slowly, and tentatively, completely and totally unsure of himself—to wrench meaning from so fragile a contact.

One hour, two, I wrote in such a manner. But then I became more sure of myself; the story began to take real shape. Biting, satiric, the words screamed "hypocrisy" at all the fictional church-goers, who weren't fictional at all. A lampooning, yes, but not with something as heavy and clumsy as a whaling harpoon—I punctured pretensions with the exactness of a laser. I had this church service cut up so fine that you had to step back for a moment, see the whole thing in its entirety, and then gently blow—and watch as the whole structure collapsed with the gentlest breath, a billion pieces of sin, confetti-like, where just before there had stood the portrait of sanctimoniousness. The holy became the unholy in a wink (wink) of an eye.

Again, as with my previous work on the slow death of nice people, I'd have to go back and edit a bit, polish so as to bring out the shine even more. But that would be a small matter. The story as such was now told. And after just a few moments, I had the title.

"The Divine Service"

I heaved a sigh of relief, as if a great weight had been lifted. As I looked up from the computer screen, I realized darkness blanketed the apartment. I checked my watch—9:30. I must have been working like a man possessed. I had written through lunch and dinner, never a clue, nor a thought, about the time. But, though a bit hungry, I found myself more sleepy than anything else. And so I went to bed, finally able to rest.

7

Anything for a laugh. I heard the doorbell at seven, opened it, and there stood the devil, bells and all. Kind of cute, in a way. A small bell hung from his ear; when he flicked it, a high pitched tingling went off. A very casual tan sports jacket had tiny bells for cuff links. He wore a shirt that had a little liberty bell as the logo—I had never seen that brand before, so I assumed he custom made the look just for me. And to top it all off, or bottom things out, he had on a pair of bell bottom jeans.

I just shook my head as he laughed.

"I keep my word," he said, explaining the get-up. "Here with bells on. Ready to go?"

I grabbed my jacket. By October it can be cool around Chicago, so it's always best to have a jacket. And it's not called the "Windy City" for nothing. So I went out prepared. Without even thinking about it, we went to Orly's.

Jerry greeted us by the door, and I indicated a little table in the corner would be nice; I liked being where the devil and I could speak freely. I saw a couple of old friends that Jill and I used to hang out with. I threw up my hand in a friendly greeting. They waved me over, but I just shook my head and mouthed "another time."

"Good writing yesterday?" the devil asked.

"Surprisingly good," I said. "Wore me out, though.

"I think it's time to strike," he said. "Whip those two pieces into shape, go ahead and send them out." He winked at me. "I've got inside information at a couple of places where I think you'd like to have your pieces placed. Good places. Real writer stuff." Then, in a conspiratorial whisper, he leaned across the table and said, "Lack of good manuscripts. They're going to have to publish slim if they can't pull in a couple more good stories."

"I'm listening," I said.

"I think 'The Divine Service' is probably okay as is. That needs to be sort of raw, in a way, almost like exposed flesh."

It no longer surprised me that the devil knew what I had been up to, had been thinking, had written. Omniscient, almost. That's how I had come to think of him.

I did wince, however, at his comparing my work to exposed flesh.

He caught my thought.

"Timothy, you've got to tear back the skin a little bit to see what's underneath. Skin-deep writing isn't going to make anyone sit up and pay attention to you. Don't wince. Don't be ashamed. It's a fine story, and it tells the truth."

I shrugged my shoulders. Maybe I had winced because the service itself hurt me so badly.

"So, we'll ship that one off as is, but we have to do it tomorrow. Just three months from ship date, so even in their dire straights, these publishers are on the verge of sending material off to the typesetters. Mail it express, tomorrow, so it's there by Wednesday. My guess is that you'll have a call by Friday, and you'll be in."

"You're certainly confident," I observed.

"Not confident," the devil corrected, "simply well informed."

The waiter headed our way, only to be called back by Jerry. After a quick word, the waiter returned.

Nice as he could be. I ordered quiche (I always ordered quiche there; some folks would call that a rut, but I call it knowing what you like); and I requested salad and water for the devil. Almost like a date, him telling me what he'd like, me ordering for him. At least in this regard—having the cash to pay—the devil relied on me. And I didn't mind. The help I was getting on my writing was invaluable.

After the order had been placed, the devil took on a no-nonsense, back-to-business approach. "But your first story," he said, as if we hadn't been interrupted, "needs work, just a little. You can do it in a couple of hours."

"What's that?" I asked.

"Make it southern," he said. "Give it a little dialect—not too much, because a little goes a long way. A hint of difference, that's all that's necessary. Make the setting explicitly southern. We're going to send this to a southern magazine; you're from the South, and it's entirely appropriate. What other region in the country is still caught up in any semblance of politeness, where there's some value to being 'nice,' at least as a veneer to cover up the ugliness of southern emotion? My God, it's as if they don't realize the war's been over a long time."

I liked the idea. And I knew exactly what the devil was talking about. A thin film of politeness, of being nice, applied to even the most hateful thoughts, was an art form where I came from. You could say the most awful thing about a person, but as long as you said it nicely, and somewhere threw in a "poor thing" or a "bless her heart," then you could engage in any sort of character assassination and not an eyebrow would be raised.

I could make it work. Almost hated to have to sit through dinner, I wanted to go and start immediately.

But sit through dinner I did. The devil occasionally hummed to himself; sometimes told a joke. Most were groaners. "Two nuts walked into a bar," he said. "One was assaulted."

I learned not to encourage him, though I smiled inside. He so enjoyed the jokes he told, and all of them were clean. He didn't go in for vulgarity, not usually.

He tried harder.

"A man walked into a bar." He paused for dramatic effect. "He said 'ouch.'" He got a real chuckle out of that one, and I got tickled just watching him. His attitude was funnier than anything he said, or most anything.

No, no raunchy jokes. The closest I ever heard him come to anything approaching inappropriate—and this was mild—was that night.

We sat there at the end of the meal. Just like last time, the devil mostly seemed to move his food around on his plate. I couldn't even remember him taking a bite of his salad, though I assumed he had. Either that or he was bad to play with his food.

An older lady, very nicely dressed, "portly" being the word best to describe her, even though a woman, walked by us. We were in the most private area, but it happened to be the area one walked through to get to the washrooms.

She walked primly, tightly. I glanced up. Her face was red. I thought to myself, "I think she really has to go."

And just as she walked by the table, she passed gas. Not much, just a toot. And that was what it sounded like; a mangled attempt to get sound from a brass horn.

I know the lady had to have been dying. Older, dressed as she was. No, this was no public farter. I'm sure she felt she had disgraced herself and would probably never come to this restaurant again, never visit the place of her humiliation.

Those random, silly thoughts rushed through my head in an instant. She had barely passed us when the devil said, his voice serious as funeral fees, "And the last trumpet shall sound."

I died laughing.

The lady hurried on to the washroom, degradation dogging her every step. I turned red, I laughed so hard. The devil sat there innocently, as if, every day, the sound of flatulence carried apocalyptic overtones. By the time I finally calmed down a bit, he shrugged his shoulders and asked, "What?"

That started it all over again.

I don't think the woman thought the situation all that funny. When she came back by, I was still laughing, with the devil giving me these little looks every time I almost had things under control. She huffed and puffed her way past my table, as if to blow my little house of laughter away. She immediately gathered up her husband, and they left.

On the one hand, I felt badly; on the other hand, it was so funny.

I laughed so hard on the way out—the devil kept making little trumpet sounds—that I'm sure a number of customers thought I was drunk. Because I didn't want to be thought a troublemaker, I left an especially large tip, and a note saying how nice everything was. But I still think Jerry was glaring as I stumbled out the door, drunk on good humor.

We walked back to my place, and almost as if it were understood, I went to the computer keyboard and pulled up the "slow death of nice people" file. The devil relaxed in a chair and turned the TV on.

I worked for a couple of hours then decided to take a break.

"What'cha watching?" I asked as I sat down.

"It's a bunch of thugs figuring out how to snuff somebody out, I think is how they say it," the devil replied.

"Must be cable," I said, "that's pretty raunchy language."

"Indeed," the devil replied. "Crude thoughts expressed by crude people. And they're so uncreative. My goodness," he said, a half-smile slipping across his countenance as he said it, "give me good, upstanding folk trying to get out of a mess. That's when you see creativity. They're so wound up about being 'good,' they'll go to quite diabolical extremes to make sure their good names aren't tarnished."

I nodded my head, not really agreeing, just acknowledging that he had spoken.

The TV clicked off.

"Done?" he asked.

"Hit a bit of a rough spot I wouldn't mind going over with you," I said. I was wondering if I had gone too much over the top in describing the gore after the nice guy finally snapped.

"Yeah, let me see," the devil said. He followed me back to the computer, reading over my shoulder just the last couple of pages.

"Maybe a bit," he finally said. "This may be a case where less is more. Give hints at the horrors committed; draw an outline. Let your reader fill in the color."

After a moment's thought, I agreed.

So I began to rewrite, and the devil went back to watching TV. I don't know what channel he had it on, but there seemed to be an awful lot of bad things happening, judging by the wailing and gnashing of teeth, so to speak, that I heard. Turns out, I should have paid more attention to what was up—blinded, I guess, by my own ambition and work. I didn't connect the evil on the screen with the one sitting watching it. So many signs that I missed—probably because I was looking only at me and what I was doing and what I would become and what I would accomplish. So self-oriented, I suppose, that I thought, since he was being so nice to me, how bad could he be? Well, I guess the old cliché is true—there's none so blind as those who will not see. I was blind as a bat. Too much involved in *my* work.

"Finished!" I cried after about only forty-five minutes more of rewrite.

"Let's get ready to send these babies off, then," he replied. He hopped up and came and stood by me. "I've got to get going, actually," the devil said. "Some things have just come to my attention that I need to, shall we say, 'shepherd' along." He laughed, a private joke I thought, but then he explained. "Get it? Shepherd along? Latin for 'shepherd' is 'pastor.' You know that," he said, winking at me, giving me credit for my years of Latin study. "Never thought of Lucifer as a pastor before, have you?" he asked. "But I am, in every real and meaningful sense of the word. I am humanity's true shepherd."

I started to ask him what he meant, but he interrupted me. "Really, I do have to go. But I know you'll write a first-class intro letter for that fine manuscript of yours." And I was so caught up with the possibility of publishing in a good venue, I dropped the question—and forgot about it completely. I had to get back to my little world, not humanity's.

"Where do I send these things?" I asked, a little panicky that he was going to let me finish on my own. But everything was okay.

"Get on the net," the devil instructed, already heading for the door. "Find out submission info for *Ploughshares* and the *Oxford*

American. Some places take only electronic submission, a few holdouts take only paper, some take either. I assume you know the southern piece should go to *Oxford*?"

"Are you sure?" I asked, a bit stunned. This was jumping to the front of the line. Both great magazines, with *Ploughshares* serving as the really high-brow literary magazine. I kinda thought the devil meant for me to work my way up, spend a little time learning my craft. After all, besides gift books, I really hadn't done much writing—I was the kind of guy who always talked about writing. And any attempts I had made went toward the aborted Great American Novel, never toward a short story. My God! It took years of practice, I knew, to get the short story form down just right. I couldn't just slap something together and expect it to be seriously considered by the type of venues the devil suggested.

"Believe me," the devil said. "They will take them. They're good, and they need them. Just be sure to say that a mutual friend—and they'll know who—directed you their way."

And with that, he was gone.

I went through and got addresses. A nervous energy shook my insides. These were honest-to-goodness the real deal. Only real writers got published in the likes of these magazines. And I might be one of them. I shivered all over. My first step toward being something other than a rich hack, something more than a lucky sonofabitch with one cute idea. A writer who plumbed the depths of human nature, its existence and experience. That's what I was going to be.

I wrote up a good letter to go with each manuscript. When it came time to address the 9 x 12 envelopes, I didn't use a mailing label spit effortlessly from a laser printer. Instead, I hand addressed each, lovingly using a script I had learned many years before, a variation on a medieval style I had picked up when doing Latin paleography. Calligraphy came to me easily, like the little doodads I did as illustrations for my books.

I let the ink dry, then ran my hand across each of them. It looked odd in a way. The *Oxford American* had left its home in Oxford, Mississippi, where the ghost of William Faulkner whispered, no doubt, his musings in the ears of the many editors who had sought over the years to maintain the tradition of southern fiction. I wondered if the spirit of a man like Faulkner would be up to traveling over to Arkansas, where editors would continue to sit and think through the jumbled wreck of southern tradition and print it in a magazine called the *Oxford American* but which no longer came from Oxford.

These and other thoughts continued to ramble through my head as I made my way for bed. I set my alarm clock for early, wanting to be the first person at the post office. Express mail, that's how it'd go. A part of me, of my soul, of its wrestling with *the state of humanity*, at least that part that could reasonably fit within the black ink of letters, would be airborne and on its way to the wider world all around.

8

We wheeled down I-90, radio blaring, on our way to Gary, Indiana. The devil was in the mood for country. I don't know if he tinkered with the electronics or what, but he had my system louder than I had ever had it—and I was pretty sure we weren't going to blow a speaker.

"I feel lucky," he devil sang, his voice equaling the radio decibel for decibel. He matched Mary Chapin Carpenter, note for note, word for word.

At one point, the devil placed his hand on my thigh, a rather intimate gesture for him. I turned and looked—and had to laugh. He had morphed into Lyle Lovett—just at that point in the song where Chapin says that ol' Lyle has his hand on her thigh. After a quick grin, the devil turned back into JFK Jr. and kept belting out the words.

After the song finished, he turned the volume down a bit so we could talk.

"How about you, my dear Timothy? Feeling lucky tonight?"

"About as lucky as I've ever felt in my whole life," I replied, then I let out a whooping noise, holding my hand up, making a fist, and waving it around.

"No tricks, right?" I asked the devil. "Just inside information?"

"That's right," the devil replied. "I knew they needed something; I knew the deadlines. But they don't run things that'll embarrass them. You're in because you deserve to be in."

I let out another whooping noise, something I probably hadn't done so loudly since high school football games.

After a bit, my yelling bled off my excess energy. At that point, I just sat and shook my head.

"I can't believe it. *Ploughshares* and the *Oxford American*, both taking my pieces, both on the same day."

"Did you send an email off to that so-called agent of yours?" the devil asked.

"Darned tooting," I said, although smiling as I said it. Since starting graduate school those many years ago, I had worked hard not to let any homely expressions escape my lips. I didn't want to seem backwards. But I said it now, and it felt good, and it felt right.

"Told him about getting both my short stories published, told him my career was going to take a shift toward the serious, and told him he'd better start figuring out a way to help me 'achieve the full potential of my literary prowess.'" It sounded a bit pompous, but the devil had used the phrase, I liked it, and so I worked it into my email. "Or else, I'd have to take my millions of dollars in sales *and* my high-falutin' literary success to someone who would be in a position to 'facilitate' my advancement in the world of letters." Again, I threw in a few words the devil had said in talking with me, letting him know I'd paid attention and appreciated his help.

"Good for you, dear boy," the devil replied. "About time that old bag started earning some money instead of simply taking yours."

I nodded vigorously in agreement.

"Man, I do feel lucky," I said.

"No place better to go then," the devil replied.

After about a twenty-minute drive or so, we exited off Cline Avenue and headed toward the river boat. The way I felt, I knew I'd be playing it, not it me. I was a winner in every way. Almost as if neon radiated out my pores, flashing "winner" brighter than anything the casino could muster.

Friday's are crowded on the boat, but less so if you head off for the hundred-dollar-a-hand-minimum black jack tables. I played almost nothing else but black jack at the boat. I had a very decent head for cards, and black jack is a game where, if you play it right, the odds are almost in the player's favor, if you don't go and do something stupid. I won more than I lost, but I always played mostly for fun, so even when I lost it didn't matter. My Methodist blood kept me from playing outrageous amounts of money anyway. I never lost more than what it'd cost for a nice night out on the town for two; and that's what it was for me anyway, a nice night out.

But I walked onboard lucky in life, so I just knew I'd be lucky in cards. So off to the high-stakes table I went. No five-dollar tables for me, not on such a lucky day.

I asked the devil if he wanted to sit, but he said no, he'd just watch. The others gave me the evil eye—like I was some kind of weirdo, like I was crazy. But I wasn't going to be psyched out.

I ponied up four thousand dollars—forty times the minimum bet, which is what it takes to ride out the bad runs. Play it right, play it with the proper amount of money, and you almost always come out better than even; sometimes a lot better.

We didn't talk much, but occasionally I would look over my shoulder and wink at the devil. The night had kissed my cards; I couldn't lose. I played my usual conservative game at first, all by the book. By the end, I went wild; splitting cards I should never have split. I'd have a pair of kings showing against a nine, and I'd split them and win. Completely wild and crazy; though not really. I had a feeling, an intuition, when to play like that. And it almost always worked out for me.

The others took it in a good natured way for a while, until I started winning big time, and they started losing. Said I was taking "their" cards. Well, no, they're *my* cards until I decide to pass. That's the game. But my unusual playing did rob my neighbors, especially the guy to my left, of some cards they needed.

The language turned ugly. The dealer let it be known that the game had to stay nice or he'd call security. The guy to my left went nuts. Started betting like mad—which meant stupidly (in other words, he started betting like me; except I won, he lost).

After he'd lost about three thousand dollars (I'd won six thousand by this time), he practically jumped off his stool as if it were a hot seat. But before he turned to go, he looked me in the eye and said, "You sonofabitch."

I looked back at him, calm and serene—at peace as only a lucky man can be at peace—and said, "It's just a game, pal."

The man let out what may have been meant as a laugh, but it came out as a howl, a mad dog's frustration. The dealer signaled security, and within just a couple of seconds, men with guns were only ten paces away.

The man quickly pulled himself together, as if taking what dignity he could find and covering the most exposed parts of himself, and said to me in a perfectly monotone voice, "It's nice to know that life is just a game to some people. Must make the living of it a little easier."

And then the men with weapons quickly escorted him away. I wondered if they'd take him to some room; or if the boat would press charges for disorderly conduct. Or would it be like a TV show, and they'd throw him out the door, and he'd roll down the steps. No, I decided, that was a lawsuit waiting to happen. They wouldn't do that. And since they wouldn't treat him in quite so bad a way, for some reason, I felt a little better.

But just a little.

"Let's go," I said to the devil, gathering up my chips. "We'll cash these out and head on home."

The guy to my right, a man whose forearm was bigger than my thigh, said, "Oh, yeah, why don't I come home with you."

Why would he say that, I wondered. But the way the man glared at me made me think questions probably wouldn't be cheerfully entertained at the moment, so I just quickly took off for the nearest cashier.

We took our winnings—a little over six thousand dollars—plus the four thousand we started with and headed for the door.

"Hey," the devil said, "How about playing a slot for me?"

"Okay," I said. We wondered around a bit. I'd suggested the dollar slots, but he said it was too rich for his blood. So we went over to the quarter slots, and I slipped in a single dollar bill. I started to play more, but the devil only wanted one good spin.

"Four games or all at once?" I asked.

"How lucky you feel?" the devil asked.

"Pretty lucky," I laughed.

"Play it all at once, then," the devil said. "I love watching the slots. All that spinning around, all that hope that, out of the senseless twirling, some semblance of gain's to be found. Blind trust in nothing but luck, mostly by people who have no earthly reason to have anything but the lowest opinion of the good lady."

After that little spiel, I asked, "You sure you want to play?"

"Yea," he said, "I'm just going on. Give it a spin for me."

After the bells quit blaring, the machine spit out a receipt, and we then made our way to the cashier's window, another ten thousand dollars richer.

I ambled off the boat, not a care in the world. It wasn't the money so much—I had plenty of that. It was the winning. The feeling that I was on a roll, and nothing could stop it. I was caught up in my thoughts when the devil said, "Let's stop by here for a minute. I love this guy."

We walked into an area that offered free entertainment. An Elvis impersonator worked the crowd. The jelly roll around his stomach made even the late-years Elvis look like an Olympic athlete. When he got all shook up, he really shook. But the crowd seemed to love him—a local favorite. Probably a local boy who they all knew.

He did the whole deal, scarves and all. He'd wrap one around some woman's neck, give her a little kiss, and she'd off and start screaming like the real Elvis had just come back to life. Some of the women looked drunk; some carried the air of desperation; some were just having fun. The men that were there mostly rolled their eyes, though some of them got into the fun of it, even going so far as to dance a little with their wives or girlfriends.

I looked over to grin at the devil during "Burning in Love." His sideburns had grown long and black, he had on sun glasses, and he was singing right along.

Man, the devil likes to sing, even if it is to bad Elvis music.

Finally, the song burned the singer up. He stopped and wiped his forehead. He had sweated through his suit as if he had just spent the last eight hours out in the field gathering the crops. I'll give him this—he put all his heart could stand into his performance.

The lights lowered. Suddenly, Elvis was out into the audience, the women fawning all over him as he started a ballad. But the noise lessened the more he got into "Are You Lonesome Tonight?"

This song he actually sang well. The crowd parted in front of him. I craned my neck to see what was going on. Fat Elvis had gotten down on one knee in front of a young woman in a wheel chair. A nice face, a shy look. She shone red, embarrassed. Other women bent down by her head, whispering something, coming up from their intimate moment in great gales of laughter. They found all this funny, for some reason. Over and over, Elvis seemed to ask, Are you lonesome tonight? At the end of the song, he wrapped a scarf around the young woman's neck and gave her a little kiss on the cheek—then, pulling back for a moment, he went in whole hog, the full lip lock, on the surprised young woman. He then straightened up, walked a few paces away, then wheeled, pointing at the young woman with good humor and winking. Then he took a break.

The freak show had turned freakish, in my opinion. I let the devil know I was ready to leave.

We didn't talk much on the way home. The devil hummed a little of this and that, occasionally breaking out into some opera or another—maybe Wagner now and again, because I heard the guttural sounds of Germanic speech. I knew there were other operas in German, but I had never heard the devil do any of them but Wagner.

By the time we were back in my apartment, the twenty thousand dollars safely locked away in a safe until I could get to a bank the next morning, I felt—odd. Something troubled me about the night. I felt good on the way down; the cards practically bowed before me in worship; the one and only spin at the slots had given me more fun money than I'd ever spend; but something sat wrong.

"You need to write," the devil remarked, taking up his usual position in front of the TV.

"I don't know," I stammered. "Don't know that I feel like writing."

"You don't feel like anything else, let me assure you," the devil confidently replied. Or maybe it wasn't a reply. An order? A command? He continued. "Just sit down. Use your writer's eye. A lot went well for you, my friend; but not for a lot of other people. Don't write about your experience; write about theirs, what you saw. I think you probably picked up a lot more at a subconscious level than you realize. Try filling in their stories, why they were there, what happened to them on this Friday evening." He then turned his head away from me and clicked on the TV, yelling back over his shoulder, just for good measure, "Write!"

And I did, almost as if I had given my will up to him and did as I was told. Almost. Not quite. I found I wanted to write. I walked into the halls of my icy memory. And it was as if, for the first time, I saw something I had never really seen before—a stairway leading downward. So down I went, to explore this new landscape. And they were all there.

The dealer. The two men, the one on my right and the one on my left. There was fat Elvis, and the poor girl to whom he sang. They were lurking there, just beneath my surface memories.

They weren't as cold; not frozen. They moved a bit. I had to interpret a little about what was going on, but I did it. My fingers wore out the keys with my typing, half the time not even realizing what I was doing. Psychoanalyzing what I'd seen, forecasting future behavior, all on the fly, at a barely conscious level.

The TV blared behind me. For some reason, I found myself listening to the sounds as I explored the inner images. I wondered to myself, "What in the devil (I smiled at my secret pun) is he watching?"

It all sounded like a real soap opera. Some guy had come home and beat his wife after having lost all his money gambling. Now they'd lose their house. He kicked the dog. All the sorts of things you'd expect from someone stupid enough to bet the farm (literally) at a casino as a last-ditch effort to get out of real debt trouble. And, of course, the baby started crying.

I just shook my head and tried to keep on writing; but then I heard the man say, voice damp with alcohol, "This damn guy kept taking all my cards." I recognized the voice.

I wheeled around in my chair, jumped up, and went and stood next to where the devil sat in front of the TV. It was the man from the boat; the man who sat to my left, tossed out by security.

"What the hell . . ." I started. But the devil interrupted me, stating flatly, "Hell had nothing to do with it. He did this all to himself."

I rubbed my eyes as the real life soap opera continued. I stood there, watching a family's life fall to pieces, and I felt responsible.

"They call it gambling for a reason," the devil said, intruding on my experience of guilt. "You were lucky tonight. He wasn't. Plain and simple. Not your fault."

I just shook my head in disbelief.

"I didn't mean to ruin his life."

The devil let out a huge laugh. "Don't get too egocentric there, my dear Timothy. His life has sat on the edge of ruin since the day he was born. It's the way the world works that's to blame. Not you." He was emphatic.

I started to disagree, but the devil switched the channel. A darkened bedroom appeared on the screen.

"Is this what you've always been watching while I've worked?" I asked. I had no idea.

"Sure," the devil replied, a happy-go-lucky tone of voice. "Very interesting. Very educational. Reality TV at its best. A nice way to see the world for what it is," he said, a little verbal nudge for me, pushing me toward coming to grips with the big picture, existence splashed in lurid colors across a flawed canvas. Lately he had been hammering on that point, over and over. He had started to indicate that I had the writer's eye; now it was time to work on the writer's heart, soul. He said I needed a vision of the world, a coherent way of looking at reality; *his* way. Vision and eye would work together, he said, to transform me into the truly great writer I could be.

But for the right then and there of it all, I was less interested in the devil's philosophy and more interested in what the TV showed.

If this was reality, the devil must have had a way of monkeying with the picture. Almost as if someone on a production set had yelled, "Cue soft light," the bedroom lightened a little, so even though you could still tell it was dark, you could see now.

The devil's camera (were there spiritual grips out there, and was there a union?) panned the room, which appeared dingy in a way that the simple darkness probably didn't explain. Then a zoom shot—and we had a face, a nice face, though a bit shy in its countenance. The woman in the wheelchair. I saw the fat-Elvis scarf wrapped around her neck.

Moving in even closer, the camera caught a tear running down the woman's cheek while she noiselessly mouthed the words, "Are you lonesome tonight?" A slow nod of the head seared her lonesomeness onto my mind's eye, my writer's eye. Terribly lonesome. And I saw a brief flash—intuition or the devil?—of a past, a young energetic girl whose life was radically, awfully changed by a drunk driver. And so lonesome now. Longing for a past life that would never be more than an imagined future, the girl continued to gently cry and mouth the words of fat Elvis. I now saw how cruel it had all been, from her perspective. A goading, a mocking, in public, with her so-called friends enjoying themselves as she shrunk into herself at every word of the song. But she couldn't get up and run away.

The camera panned down. A gun lay in the girl's lap. She began stroking the barrel. And then, out loud, she began to sing to the gun, "Are you lonesome tonight?"

In slow motion, she brought the gun up toward herself, continuing to sing, stroking the grey metal. Then she closed her eyes, gently brought the end of the barrel up to her lips and softly kissed the end of the gun, caressing the aiming bead with her lips, feeling the cold roundness, knowing it as she worked her way full circle around the end of the gun with light butterfly kisses.

Then, I heard her say, breathlessly, "You don't have to be lonesome anymore." And as if the gun were a lover, she took in the barrel with an open-mouthed kiss.

"NO!" I screamed, rushing to the screen. I started to rock the set back and forth, as if I had my arms firmly placed on the young woman's shoulders, trying to shake sense into her.

The screen went blank.

"Timothy," the devil said, "it's a pretty fragile process, getting a good picture like that." Reproof peppered his words.

"Did she do it?" I asked, frantic, beside myself.

"Probably not," the devil said, completely uninterested now that the picture had disappeared.

"How do you know?" I demanded.

"She's been in these moods before," he replied. "I don't think tonight's the night, though I thought *I'd* like to kill myself after just a few songs by that guy." He laughed, but I didn't.

"You don't care, do you?" I asked, my voice flat, just like my insides. Whatever buoyancy of good feeling had inflated my spirits all day, it had all gone now. "It's a game to you, isn't it?" I asked, trying to throw the words at him like an accusation, but mostly sounding a tad petulant.

"Whatever it is," the devil said, getting up from his seat and heading for the door, "it isn't a game."

He let himself out. But as the door closed behind him, he said, "Write, Timothy, write. Use this. She's not dead, although you have no reason to think she's better off because of that. Naive still. But do what you can with it. Work."

I stood there in disgust—at him, at myself, at God, who knows?—for some time after the door closed. Finally, I went over, locked up for the night, and surprised myself. I walked back over to the computer and started keying in like crazy.

9

The devil and I sat over dinner, celebrating my latest success. I couldn't believe how quickly the *Tin House* picked up my story, "Fat Elvis Kills." I still wondered how the manuscript ended up quite so hard, edgy. I had been so upset when I sat down to write, wondering what would happen to that poor girl. Yet the story contained no sentimentality; indeed, the girl came off rather badly, in some ways. The story was, I have to admit, a bit mean spirited. The devil's words had stuck with me—was I sure she was better off for not having pulled the trigger?

But the mood, rather than introspective, was celebrative. I had already gotten fan letters for "The Divine Service" and "The Slow Death of Nice People." Invitations to write had started appearing in my mail box. My agent had a number of houses interested in a novel (the real "quality" writing of the short stories and the extraordinary commercial success of my gift books had a few ready to make an advance on the spot). Life, in other words, was good. And now "Fat Elvis" was headed for publication—and soon. They liked the piece so well they bumped someone else from the lineup. That's status; that's respect. I loved it.

"A novel, Timothy," the devil said, his voice as excited as I had ever heard it. "A bestseller would really put you on the map. Just a little more work, and I think you're ready for it."

"What kind of work?" I asked as I slipped some of Orly's great quiche into my mouth.

"You've got the eye; the last story has shown you have the heart, unafraid to put down the truth of things without pulling away because of sentimentality. Vision. That's all that's left. A consistent worldview, a comprehensive vision of reality. A filter by which the work of your eye, heart, and hands will always have the Timothy stamp; a way people will have of instantly recognizing your work."

"Your vision," I replied, sure that that's what we were leading up to.

"My vision," the devil declared. "But not just mine. The vision of countless others. Those who see the world for what it is. Maybe not Shakespeare, but Macbeth had the vision, didn't he? 'Life *is* a tale told by an idiot,' especially if the teller is some lame-brained theist who wants to cozy up with God and say how nice things are. Nice!" He nearly spat out the word. "Darwin had it right; nature red in tooth and claw, and nothing more natural than the human race itself." He had talked himself very quickly into a sort of fury, his face shining red.

"Sartre understood. So did Faulkner. Peruse your Norton anthologies, see who's there, Timothy. Not *my* view, not really. Simply the *only* view, if one looks with an objective eye."

He sat there for a moment, looking out the window, as if lost in thought.

"Why do you like Wagner so much?" I asked him. "Does he capture the vision you're so keen on?" I brought it up because we couldn't get through a day without him singing a snippet here or there from one of the *Ring* operas.

"I like the music," the devil replied. "And I like to see how the world falls apart because of greed. There's death, destruction. A tragic ending brought about in part because of the foolishness of the gods. I see it everywhere, in all times."

I thought about that for a moment. Then I said, "But you sometimes also talk about the Norse vision, too, and you seem to appreciate it. A version at odds with what Wagner does."

"Oh yes," the devil said, his full attention back on me. "Let's not confuse the two things, which I think you may have done when we first met. I like Wagner as music, and I appreciate the themes of the *Ring* cycle. But that's not really the same as the original Norse vision, is it?"

I simply sat silent, waiting for him to continue.

"I like the Norse stories because of the principles the gods hold," the devil said. "In Wagner, they really just represent the worst of human nature; and the bungling part seems to me to reflect pretty accurately the effects of you-know-who." The devil's eyes arched upward. There were times—and this seemed to be one of them—that the devil didn't care to use the word "God."

"But the Norse vision, in some ways, that's what I'm all about," the devil went on, becoming animated as he talked, his eyes lighting up, a hint of satisfaction lifting his voice. "Think about it. You got these guys, and they know the big day is coming. Ragnarok. The twilight of the gods. The evil forces will win. The earth will be destroyed. And they know they will lose. And yet," he said, slamming his fist down on the table, "they fight. Why do they continue to prepare for a battle they cannot win, against a foe they know will overcome them, under the auspices of an All-father god who will turn around, as soon as the world goes poof in flames of destruction, and recreate the world—including all the baddies that caused the trouble? A general amnesty for those who don't in any way deserve it. Yet Odin and Thor and Tyr and the whole lot struggle on. Why?"

I simply shrugged my shoulders. I didn't know why. Norse mythology really wasn't my thing.

"I'll tell you why," the devil said with absolute confidence. "Because what they were doing was *right*. And they did what was right, the consequences be damned."

I almost laughed, but not quite. Instead, I asked the devil, "Are you serious?"

"Indeed I am," he replied, sitting up straighter, prouder. "They did the right thing in the face of circumstances that worked against them in every way. They are the noble ones. They are the ones who deserve the title 'God' rather than the pathetic 'All-father' figure." He snorted as he said "All-father," and I almost thought I saw fire flare from his nostrils.

"Don't you see?" the devil asked, leaning forward, taking me into his confidence. "I am like those grand old beings. I do what I do because it is right."

I raised an eyebrow in question.

"The world's a mess, Timothy. You have divine power that abdicates its responsibilities for the creation, lets horrible things happen, and still demands affection and worship. That's wrong. Create a paradise and let folks frolic and don't make it so it can be messed up; it's not that hard. Or create a true free-will universe, and let the thing run without begging people to love you, or coercing, or cajoling. Be sovereign, be loving, be kind, be stern, but by you-know-who"—he grinned, knowing I thought to catch him saying "God" on a day he had decided to avoid the word—"be reasonable. Be fair. Make the universe so that it's a fair shake. If you're going to damn people for having free will and making mistakes, damn them. If you're going to love everybody and bend over backwards to prove it, do it. If you're going to say to folks, 'Hey, here's some intelligence and here's some power and I'm not going to constrain how you use it, but hey, use it the right way,' what's that all about?"

"These are old arguments," I said, trying to sound sophisticated. "Every theology runs into them in some form or another and deals with them."

"Where the *hell*," he said, emphasizing the word, "do you think they picked up those arguments?"

"You?" I asked, though it really wasn't a question.

"Me," he said flatly. And then he retreated into himself for a few moments, as if thinking. He had really gotten going, I thought. Maybe he sat there trying to pull himself together. I didn't quite know.

In a low voice, he finally spoke. "You know, Origen was right in a way." I quickly ran through my mental file on Origen: third-century thinker, steeped in Platonic thought, did lots of interesting things concerning exegesis of the Bible, condemned as a heretic for some pretty interesting ideas. Like the notion that the devil, finally, would be saved, as would everything in creation. A type of universalism; Origen allowed for a hell, just not its eternity. Finally, everything would, of its own free will, turn back to God.

"How so?" I asked.

"I could go back," he sniffed, as if the very thought were beneath him. "Standing invitation. Any time I want. A few conditions. Not many really. He's always asking, Come on back, buddy, let's patch things up, you and me."

"Why don't you?" I asked.

"Because he gave me free will," the devil said, sighing as he said it. "And frankly, I just don't like him. I don't like what he's done. I don't like the way he thinks. I don't want to be anywhere around him."

That surprised me. I found myself wandering if this could possible be true, that the devil could just waltz right back into heaven. And he simply chose not to do so.

"Free will," the devil reiterated. "To have free will means that *I get to choose* with whom I associate; it means at least that or it means nothing at all. And I choose to stand with those who choose to disassociate themselves from the Almighty. It's our right. If we have true free will, it *is* our right."

"I'm a bit confused, I guess," I said.

"I'm free to think he's mucked things up something dreadful; more than that, I'm free to stand apart from him in protest. That's what I do. When it comes right down to it, that is the fundamental right of every sentient being. To choose *not* to be on his side. And he does everything he can to run rough shod over that one fundamental right in this existence that he created in the first place."

The devil leaned back, a look of determination on his face. "I am the moral center of the universe," he declared, "because true morality involves true choice, and I guard that freedom of choice at its very root. By being what I am."

I have to admit, I had never thought of any such thing in my life, but once the devil had iterated his position, it seemed perfectly plausible; in fact, perfectly reasonable, logical.

"So, Origen got it about half right," the devil declared. "It is possible for me to enter heaven." He paused, then he flashed a fierce grin at me. "But, as you people so quaintly say, it'll be a cold day in hell before I do so."

I sat there, nodding my head, recognizing the strength, maybe even the justice, of the devil's point of view.

In fact, I was so wrapped up in thinking about it, I jumped when a hand was laid on my shoulder.

"Timothy, everything okay?" It was a friend of mine—actually more a friend of Jill's, but we had always gotten along.

"Oh, sure," I said, shaking my head a little, as if emerging from a fog of thought.

He gave me a funny look. "You seem a little, I don't know, on edge a bit, you think?"

"No," I said flatly. What was the deal here?

"All righty," he said, winking his eye and patting my back. "Just wanted to check." Then he walked off.

"What's up with your friends, Timothy?" the devil asked.

"Don't know, don't care," I replied. The way he had looked down on me, pity flooding his eyes, had ruffled a few feathers. Was everything okay! That bozo didn't have a clue about how okay everything was, me on the verge of major success, commercial and literary, where with the money would also come a great deal of respect, all because of my abilities.

"Let's get out of here," I said, throwing some money down on the table, not even wanting to have to fool with a waiter.

"Sure," the devil replied. "Plus, given our chat, I've got a little TV for you to watch, just so you see the things I see."

The walk back to the apartment passed mostly in silence.

Once there we made ourselves comfortable—which meant, for me, making a little popcorn. I hadn't finished my meal at Orly's, so I didn't feel quite satisfied. Besides, we were going to watch TV, and I thought a little popcorn might go well with our entertainment for the night.

"You going to show me some really horrible thing?" I asked. The devil just sat down and pointed his finger. A picture began to take shape on the screen.

"You know what's funny?" the devil asked. "Your race is an odd lot, though I think I'm starting to understand you better."

"What do you mean?" I asked.

"All sorts of terrible things happen here," he said, meaning the entire earth, as far as I could tell. "Sometimes thousands of people die at a time. Fierce battles are fought. Or hundreds of thousands slowly starve. Yet, what gets everybody's dander up is a story on an individual—if it's a child, all the better. People will sit back and literally watch boatloads of people die, but if a little tyke is in trouble or has been mistreated, there's this great cry for something to be done."

He had a point.

"But I get it now," the devil said. "You people really have to put a face to tragedy, boil it down so that it means something to you, so that you can relate to it on an individual level."

"I think that's probably right," I said.

"Just like when you wrote 'The Divine Service.' You think you would've written the same kind of story if I had shown you genocide in progress somewhere around the world instead of a bunch of self-absorbed teens setting their sights on the outgroup girl of the week?"

I thought honestly about that.

"No," I said, "probably not. To see hundreds of people die seems so unreal, too like all the movies you see where battles rage and whole blocks of actors fall dead to the ground. But to see a young girl, kneeling in church, alone despite the crowd, so wanting to be accepted, and so obviously not. Not real death, but some little part of her soul dying, nonetheless. Such a little thing; but such a big thing. That just hits a chord in a way the other doesn't, I guess. It's something I can relate to."

I searched my mind for some bit of trivia I once heard. Then it came.

"Stalin once said that the death of one is a tragedy, the death of a million is a statistic." I waited for a moment, assuming he'd take some credit for Stalin and his words.

"That so?" the devil responded. He didn't seem much interested.

"I figured you gave him that line," I said, only half joking.

"No," he said. He seemed to ponder things a bit.

"That's what I think, too" the devil agreed. "Makes a great deal of sense of the way humans think." As if making an important decision, he looked down, chin set, and eyebrow raised. "A human problem, even humanity's problem, needs a face to make it real."

After a little more thought, he declared, "So, in that spirit, let me show you something, something that goes to the heart of what I see as wrong with this whole universe."

He directed my attention to the TV screen. It showed a guy locked in his study. Over the course of the next few minutes, both his wife and children knocked on the door, but he told them in no uncertain terms to go away—he was working on his sermon, and they knew better than disturb him as he worked.

"Recognize him?" the devil asked.

I looked hard. "Yeah, I think I do. He's at the big Methodist church." Jill and I had visited the church when we first started dating, but she needed more of a formal liturgy for it to seem like "real" church to her.

"A good guy," I said. "Powerful preacher. Church does a lot of community outreach."

"Yeah, I think he probably is a good guy," the devil said. "Of course, he's like everyone else. Feels stuck at times. Like now. He's in a great big Methodist church here in Chicagoland. Making good money while doing a lot of good—not great money, but enough that he provides well enough for the wife and kids. It'd be hard to walk away from, don't you think?"

"What do you mean?" I asked.

"Well, look at the guy. Pushing fifty, two teenagers at home who have all kinds of needs, not the least of which soon will be a college education. Wife has never worked outside the home—the good traditional pastor's wife. He went straight from high school to college to seminary to parish. He's pretty sure there's nothing else in the world he could do to earn a living, at least not as good a one as he makes now."

"So what's wrong with that?" I asked.

"Look at him," the devil said.

Devil-cam zoomed in, first on the computer screen. Looked to me like a sermon on the grace of God—based on the prodigal son story—was taking shape. Then the camera pulled away, and the TV showed a close up of the minister's face. Nothing seemed unusual at first, but then I noticed the guy's nose was red. He cleared his throat. A sniffle sounded. I wondered if he had a cold.

Then I saw it.

A tear ran down his face on one side, then on the other. And I sat there and watched the minister write his sermon for about five more minutes, and the longer he wrote, the quicker the tears came.

By the time I looked away, the man was literally shaking as he tried to keep working at his keyboard.

Then the screen went blank.

"He hates it," the devil said. "He hates working at the church, he hates the staff he works with, he hates his parishioners." The devil let out a long sigh. "He really hates God, but more than anything else he hates himself for being such a hypocrite."

"What's going on with him?" I asked.

"He stopped believing in God five years ago. Or at least in the God that he thought at one time had strangely warmed his heart. He feels alone, isolated. Yet, God doesn't come down and say, 'Hey buddy, cheer up. You're doing a great job. I appreciate it. Let me sit and keep you company a while.' That's all the guy wants. A sense of God's presence. Hasn't felt it in forever. Now he doesn't really believe anymore, but he has to churn out the sermons, week after week. Always with tears in his eyes. Always calling himself names. Thinking he has no integrity, no intellectual honesty. Swapping God-talk for money. He's good at it; gets rewarded pretty well for speaking it. But he's dying on the inside."

I thought about what the devil said. All the times I sat in front of a keyboard, typing twaddle. I hated it. It was expected; it made me money; but it had starting killing me on the inside, too. Then I thought of having to sit and do something like that, every single week, never getting a break, week after week, year after year. What a sad life. And it made me sad, for a little while. Then it made me angry. Why set up a world like this, where an obviously good man has to sell his soul to make a living, and not to the devil, but to the God who demanded much and returned little?

"I need to think this through, write something up, not for publication, but just to deal with it," I said as I got up and headed for the computer. It took me a second to realize I was alone in the room; the devil had vanished.

Just as well; I had work to do. Celebration time was over.

10

"Damnable Lies" went to the *New Yorker* on the devil's advice. Well, why not? Time for a reality check, time to see if I stood ready for prime time. Just the fact that it was finished was surprising enough. I started out thinking I wouldn't submit the piece on the crying minister anywhere, but the more I worked on it, the more the writing took shape as a story. As I worked through what the devil had shown me, the pastor's personal history and his web of relationships developed in my mind; his psychological profile appeared as if downloaded from some great idea computer in the sky. I wrote the entire piece in one long twenty-nine-hour marathon session.

A couple of weeks passed. I found myself wanting to get out of the apartment, so I decided on a trip to State Street. For as long as I had lived in Chicago, I had traveled north from Hyde Park to downtown to partake of the most commercialized display of Christmas ever invented—the decorations along State Street. Marshall Fields had been serving up Christmas window displays for over a century. Of course, they went out of business, but Macy's continued the tradition when they took over the building on State. I loved the windows, thoroughly enjoyed the decorations up and down the street, and always made it into the store to see the Great Tree in the Walnut Room. Commercial or not, it was magical; maybe because, in fact, it was commercialism run amok that I found it so captivating. The twinkle in young children's eyes on Christmas morning, after all, probably comes more from the ministrations of Saint Nick than meditation on the Christ child. At least, it did for me, if being honest.

So downtown I went. It was, of course, cold. But mid-December cold in Chicago couldn't keep away Christmas shoppers and window gawkers. In fact, a mid-December cold was rarely of concern to true Chicagoans. Still, I dressed in many layers, because, after all, I was not a true Chicagoan.

I began visiting the various Christmas windows. I always wondered how long it took to create the displays. I'm not very good with my hands, so I can't make things, I can't arrange things, and so the creation process of such wonderful scenes appeared mysterious to me. For the person in charge of displays, maybe it was just another job. For me, it might as well have been Santa's elves in there, creating visual enticements that gently rocked the senses into a vague sense of good will mixed with desire.

The first window featured a carriage of candy-cane material seeming to float along on pink cotton candy. It was a sweets-themed window, and I reached into my pocket for a lemon drop to suck on. The displays were already working their magic.

Next I took a step back into time. A little girl, dressed as if she had stepped out of the fifties, stood in front of an oversized mailbox, all decorated, standing ready to receive her letter clearly addressed to Santa. A Christmas tree in the background and a snow-covered street created an atmosphere of anticipation as the little girl's hand held out the envelope, almost to the receptive mail slot, which would whisk her letter away, her wishes brought directly before the man in red. Her cheeks were pink, her eyes bright, and her hair curled perfectly. An innocent smile graced her face. "This is Christmas," I thought.

The next scene I found a bit confusing at first. It was on a track, a revolving display. And it was religiously themed. That surprised me; didn't think retail stores had run such explicitly Christian scenes in quite some years. Yet it was, and an odd thing it was, too. It wasn't a crèche scene, but a precursor to that—Mary and Joseph's trip to Bethlehem. Joseph walked alongside Mary as she rode on a donkey, moving through what was meant to be a middle-eastern looking environment, which meant, mostly, sand and a couple of palm trees against a painted background of barren hills. A modest bump in her middle announced Mary's state of expectancy. A plaque in front of the display read "Mary and Joseph Travel to Bethlehem."

For some reason, I found the window unsettling. After disappearing from view for a few seconds, Mary, Joseph, and the donkey came wheeling around the display again. This time Mary was considerably more pregnant; almost too pregnant. I was shocked. I couldn't figure out what the store was peddling in this case. I looked at the caption on the plaque again. It read, "Seems almost vulgar, doesn't it?"

I shook my head, the moving track hid the little family from view once again, and then I looked down at the plaque a third time. I couldn't believe my eyes: "Like a Virgin."

I looked up and saw an absurdly pregnant Mary sitting on the donkey, but the poor donkey's legs were bent, giving way to the weight he bore. But it wasn't Mary sitting there any longer. It was Madonna. In full white corset mode—except the corset was ripping apart at the seams.

Then beside me, humming the song that made Madonna super famous, was the devil.

"That," I said emphatically, "is gross." I turned my back on Madonna/Mary before I saw parts popping out I didn't want to see.

"Why so?" the devil asked casually. "Just a little reminder what birth entails."

"Maybe so," I replied, "but still, gross."

I began to walk away from Macy's, no longer in the holiday mood. The devil's antics had caused the holiday magic to dissipate.

"Hey, just having a bit of fun." Then his tone turned serious. "Since you're done here, why don't we stroll down to the Art Institute? Got something I want you to see. Goes along with what you just saw."

Okay, the notion that something at the Art Institute could in any way go along with what I had just seen seemed intriguing. A little bit of the holiday cheer reemerged, and I said, "Sure, why not. There's other decorations to look at along the way."

We took off at a fair clip; it was, after all, December, no matter the brave face the native Chicagoans put on it. We walked down State, took a left on Washington, then a right on Michigan. We passed the Fine Arts building; I had done a little teaching there as a graduate student through the university's continuing ed program. Loved the feel of it, young musicians practicing, design artists hard at work, starving scholars hawking their wares, that is, their subject areas. Then we crossed the street.

We were in luck. It was Thursday. Thursdays are free days after 5 p.m. We were a bit early, but an employee with the Christmas spirit decided to let us go on through, maybe because I said something about it being nice to be inside away from the cold.

The old fellow laughed. "Cold, you say?" He gave me the once over. "Not from here, are you?"

"Been here some years now," I replied, smiling back at him. He just laughed again and stated, "Not from here." He waved us through.

The devil seemed to know where he was going, so I just followed him.

"Now, back to what you saw back at Macy's. All natural, right?"

I just shrugged my shoulders.

"Hey, I didn't make things the way they are," he said. "Just pointing out the little absurdities sometimes."

"What absurdity?" I asked.

"Well, childbirth," he said, as if it were the most obvious thing in the world.

"What about it?" I asked. "Gotta get born somehow."

"Yes," the devil replied, "but why like *that?* Sure, I get it that you folks are all about the material, girl." He winked at me, letting me in on his great sense of humor, bringing attention to it. I just stared blankly.

"Oh, come on, Timothy!" he said, a hint of exasperation slipping into his voice. "Material. Girl. Madonna. You just saw her in the display window!"

"Oh, yeah," I laughed, actually a bit surprised that I hadn't picked up on the little word play. "I really am cold. Slowing down the ol' mental reflexes, I guess."

The devil raised an eyebrow, letting me know that the cold might not have that much to do with my mental agility.

"Anyway," he continued, "let's talk about the flesh. You're a creature of flesh. Surely, you've wondered why life in the flesh has to be so, what's the word? Crappy."

"Well, I don't know that it's that, all the time, anyway."

"Sure it is," the devil said. "Pain, suffering. Even in that most precious of moments—the birth of new life. Especially then."

"Well, that's just . . . life." It was my turn to wink at him.

"But think, think! It's almost like a bad joke. Yeah, you get the little ball of joy, but only after a bundle of pain. Erasmus was right, after all."

"How was Erasmus right?" I asked. "And did you make him 'right?'"

"Oh, we talked, of course," the devil acknowledged. "Enjoyed working with him on *Praise of Folly*. You know it, right?"

I nodded.

"Lots of fun, that. Great satire. But the line of interest here is this—he wrote that the only way your species continued was because of the goddess Folly."

"How so?" I asked, now interested. I had read Erasmus, that great sixteenth-century Christian humanist, but I had forgotten this part.

"Simple. The only way a woman gets pregnant a second time is if Folly comes along and makes her forget the first time. Because no one, *no one*, really wants to go through childbirth a second time." Then he said, almost under his breath, "Nor the first, if sense had anything to do with it."

"Fine," I agreed, "childbirth is hard. What are you saying?"

"Only this," the devil retorted. "Erasmus tip-toed around the issue with words. But the real issue is this: not just childbirth, but the whole of bodily existence is somehow a bit, well, disgusting, degrading; in fact, revolting."

"Says you," I said. Probably not the most reasoned reply.

"Oh, not just me," he coolly replied. "Look at some of the early church theologians. A definite disdain for the body among some of them. Heck, where do you think monasticism comes from?"

"Okay, tell me more," resigned to a lecture on theology that was sure to disperse what little of the Christmas feeling I still had left.

He talked as we walked. "What about Origen? He got to the root of the problem, so to speak."

I knew where he was going. "You know, a lot scholars now think that the stories of Origen's self-castration are just that—stories, made up by his adversaries."

He took me seriously for a moment. "Yes, many think that now, but certainly not all. And you still have to deal with Eusebius, that font of information for all things early church. He says it. Most Christian scholars take his word almost as gospel, so to speak. Why balk with his story of Origen? In for a penny, in for a pound. Right?"

"Well," I stammered, trying to think of some kind of response.

"Besides," the devil asserted, "doesn't matter. I was there. He did castrate himself. And it had everything to do with a disgust of the body. Origen had a glimpse, a vision, of the truly spiritual. After that, the reality of a human body, with all that entails, became a bit hard for him to swallow. Wasn't just the sex thing, you know," he confided, "that would be a bit petty and, really, off base. It was the symbolism of the castration. It became, for him, a symbol for the process of completely subduing the flesh."

Then he stopped abruptly. "Ah, here we are."

We stood before a little exhibit, an art history lesson. Two pictures lay side by side.

"A palimpsest," he declared.

"What?" I asked.

"You know, a palimpsest," he said. I racked my brain. I should have known this.

"A reused piece of material, sometimes for writing, sometimes for drawing. You scrape the surface, reuse it. Sometimes, though, you can see what was left. Sometimes, you can peel away the new overlay, see what was underneath."

I looked again at the pictures. I guessed them to be early Renaissance.

"A commission," the devil said. "Except it went wrong. Supposed to be an Annunciation. See in the picture on the right, the overlay? The angel Gabriel is there, announcing to Mary that she's to be the mother of God, the vessel of the Incarnation. See, she looks humble, arms crossed, accepting."

I peered more closely. The devil had accurately described the picture.

"But look at what is revealed underneath the overlay; a somewhat different picture. With a little ingenuity, the right equipment, it's like getting down to the bones of a picture, especially when it's been redone."

The devil was right. Same Gabriel, same room, same Mary. Yet, in this one, though arms were crossed, it was not in submission. Instead, her head was turned, looking away, arms placed in front of her, crossed, almost in defiance; if not that, at least a defensive position, as if warding off something unwanted.

"See, the artist was made to redo it. Turn the head back toward Gabriel. Bowed. Head bowed." Then, as he so often did, he muttered to himself, "Just the way he likes it."

I was fascinated by the portrait. The rejected painting, the hidden portrait, the subversive picture, called to me. A story ran through Mary's posture, one that the official church didn't want told.

"Renunciation," the devil declared. "That's what the artist called this piece. His Mary didn't want any part of childbirth; she wanted no part of being Incarnation's vessel; she is one who considered the impending flesh-rending prospect of childbirth unbearable. She rejected it."

I saw it in her face. This drawing had a history, a story. And I saw it all, then and there.

"So," the devil asked, as if we were just standing idly about, as if I had not just been blown away by what I had seen, "what now? Other exhibits? Something else you're dying to see?"

I stood, still transfixed. I heard his voice, but it made no impact, none whatsoever.

People moved around me. There were even noises, voices, announcements, but I paid no heed. The scene before my eyes held me, crushed me, molded me, caressed me. Finally, a voice penetrated my enraptured state. "Hey, son," the old gentleman who had manned the admission window said, "finally get warm?"

I turned. "Yes, ah, I did. Thank you."

"Well," he replied, turning to leave, "closing time. Time to head back out into the cold."

I left the building and hailed a taxi. But I wasn't the least bit cold. In fact, heat seemed to radiate from me. I made it home, practically blasting through the door, catching it on the rebound, it having hit the wall hard enough to bounce back. I locked up, dropped my coat and scarf to the floor, and, with purposeful strides, made my way over to the computer. This wasn't my usual experience of frozen images. Instead, the story coursed through my mind like molten lava, burning away the self-deception of sentimentality. My fingers flew as I keyed in the title.

"Renunciation"

At that very moment, both the Christmas spirit and the December cold disappeared, turned to ash by the heat.

II

Early spring in Chicago that year was brutal—living right off the lake like I did, seems we had a ton of snow dumped on us. Of course, there was the usual snow for one of the early April White Sox games. But it was more than that—seemed as if winter didn't want to let go. Mid-April saw a combination of ten inches of snow with forty and fifty mile-per-hour winds, so some snow drifts were up over six feet.

But finally, one Friday afternoon in late April, the sun shone as if it had decided it had been sneaking around behind clouds for too long. Proud to be drenching the earth with light, just as I was proud that my work was seeing the light of day, with "Damnable Lies" coming out so quickly in the *New Yorker* after I had submitted it. The historical fiction piece, "Renunciation," landed, of all places, in the *Paris Review*. Given the kind of story it was, I thought it a long shot at best. Yet, it was now in print, ink hardly dry on the issue. I told the devil we should go do some proper celebrating: good old-fashioned drinking. "I mean to drink to my success," I said, "and success it is." I headed for the door.

And so after a lovely walk, we arrived at Jimmy's Tavern, where more beer had been spilled over dissertation drafts than probably any other place in the world. Though a lot of the university students hung out there, faculty also stopped by for drinks. Often, if faculty members and students were drinking together, that meant something good, like a successful defense of a dissertation. But just as often, you'd see some poor schlub drinking alone, trying to think through how to salvage an academic career that had crashed and burned before it ever got off the ground—academic runway catastrophes, with no fire and rescue units to help, only kegs of beer to ease the pain.

But more so than either celebration or tragedy, students came to act like students—talking theory that they had just learned in class, trying to make the new words roll off their tongues as if they themselves had coined them; having heated discussions that the average person would have neither understood nor would have cared to understand; and a large number of students hoping the greatest sex organ really was the brain and not something else—else they'd be going without.

"Great choice," the devil said as we made our way in. "I love this place."

"Been here before?" I asked.

"You kidding?" The devil replied, "Some of my best conversations and most ardent converts are intimately tied to this place, my dear Timothy."

"Well, before you go off evangelizing," I said, smiling at my little joke, "let me grab a beer. You want one?"

"Not right now," he replied. "I'll go get us a seat."

We went over next to the windows—about as lighted an area as you were going to get in Jimmy's, though the decades of grime did serve to filter out a good deal of the late afternoon sunshine.

I hoisted my beer, and the devil played along, as if he too held a mug, and we pretend clinked glasses.

I usually nursed a single beer along about all night, but for some reason, a thirst had overcome me that cried out for a foamy, bitter quenching. I drained the entire mug. A waitress came by just as I finished and asked if I wanted another. I did.

The second went down like the first. Finally feeling satisfied, the third one sat there cozy, mostly to keep me company, just an occasional sip crossing my lips.

"What's up, Timothy?" the devil asked. He seemed genuinely concerned.

"Just celebrating," I said, staring out the window.

"You have a lot to celebrate," he said. "The *New Yorker. Paris Review*. You know what this means, don't you."

I let out a sigh. "Yes, yes I do." I let the words hang in the air for a while before shooing them away with my next sentence, a more complicated sentence despite the paucity of words.

"Got a letter today," I went on. The mood immediately dimmed. I took a bigger sip of beer.

"Really?" the devil asked, content to let me tell my story instead of butting in, as he often did, showing off, making a spectacle of all the things he already knew about my life and what I was thinking and what I had been doing.

"My folks," I said, an even shorter sentence that became even more complex.

"Ah," he said, again playing the waiting game.

Finally, I spilled the beans. "I've been sending them stuff, things I've written. Kind of expected them to say something nice, congratulations, something like that."

"Fat chance, eh?" the devil said.

"Fat chance indeed," I said. "Not a word, really. Until today."

"What'd they say?"

"Just how disappointed in me they were," I said, looking into my beer. "Said they'd raised me to be a nice boy."

The devil laughed. "Did they?"

"Yep," I continued. "Said I should be using my gifts for some good thing, not writing trash that belittles religion or politeness, and certainly not writing about casinos and 'sickies,' which is how they referred to the suicidal girl in 'Fat Elvis Kills.'"

Another sigh slipped out. "They just don't get it."

"Oh, I think they do," the devil said. "They had a good idea, they thought, with Gyms for Jesus—remember, the bill due for years of love, support, blah blah blah. You wouldn't pay up. Don't be fooled, Timothy," the devil said, a hardness sweeping over his face, as if chiseled from granite, sharp and unmoving. "What you're getting now is a 'past due' bill. You didn't pay up when you could have. Despite all they've done for you, as they let you know oh so unsubtly. If you want anything from them beyond the cursory 'we love you, here's a birthday card you sonofabitch' you're going to have to cough up the dough."

Looking back on those days, the thing I hate most is how, at that very moment, I absolutely agreed with him.

"They'll die when they see the *Paris Review* piece," the devil commented.

"Unless someone down there shows it to them—pretty unlikely, if you ask me, if not down right impossible—they won't see it. I haven't sent that one because it just came out. Now I'm not going to." I sounded like a ten-year-old in a bad mood.

"And why should you?" the devil asked. "I mean, really? I know you people want your parents to be proud and all that—and we won't even get into God/humans parent complex that's the same screwed up dynamic—but finally you have to grow up." Then the devil looked at me and smiled. "And you have grown up, Timothy, as a writer, I mean. You write it as it is."

I nodded my head, vigorously agreeing.

All of a sudden, the devil slid out from behind the table and said, "Be back in a bit."

He didn't usually run off like that, but I just grabbed my beer, shrugged, and took a swallow.

I looked out the dingy window; the light had about seeped out of the day and shadows were long. A lot like my memories, I thought, long dark shadows. No doubt about it; I was brooding.

Maybe it was the brooding look that brought her over. One minute, I was sitting there stirring the cauldron of memories, parental olio, best served hot and bitter, and the next a young woman had seated herself across the table from me.

"Uh, hello," I said, I bit taken aback.

"Hi!" she said enthusiastically. She then straightened herself up in the chair while at the same time throwing her chest out toward me and then reached across with her hand, obviously ready for a handshake. So I reached over.

She grabbed my hand and shook it vigorously, intent on showing, I think, that she had a very good grip. "My name's Mindy," she said. "Mindy Turner."

"Hi, Mindy," I said, returning only a pale imitation of the smile she had flashed my way, "I'm . . ."

And before I could finish, she blurted out, "Timothy McFarland. I know." She giggled, like a high school girl, or at least like the high school girl in the imagination of every nerdishly shy high school boy who has ever lived. An inviting sound that hinted that the invitation would extend to many thereunto undreamt of (or, actually, very dreamt of) things. I felt flattered and foolish, though mostly flattered, and she hadn't even gotten beyond basic naming.

"How do you know me?" I asked.

"You're practically famous," she said, or more precisely, breathlessly enthused. Though I started to respond, I found I had nothing to say; I closed my mouth after just a few seconds, probably not that noticeable.

"I'm a grad student in American lit here at UC," she told me. "There's a class I'm taking, Contemporary Short Story. It's great. Instead of textbooks, we've subscribed to a number of literary magazines, print and online." She paused a moment for effect, then said, "We've spent a *lot* of time on some of your work."

"Really?" I asked, glad that that one word was all she needed to keep going. I liked just looking at her, watching her talk, studying her face (and her breasts, as discreetly as I could). She was a stunner.

"Yeah!" she exclaimed. "We read the recent issues of *Ploughshares* and *Oxford American*. Those stories were so—real." She reached across the table and took hold of my hand, this time not like a handshake, but gently, enticingly. "It's like you peeled all the false layers off life, like, I don't know," she giggled again, a giggle that probably would have sounded silly to any other person in the world not sitting directly across from her. "It was like layers of an onion, pulling one lie off after another, going deeper and deeper, and finally discovering that there's no core, nothing there at all."

"Well," I started to say, and then I simply shrugged my shoulders. I had no clue what to do. I had never been a ladies man; women had never chased me; more than anything, I was lucky to have ever gotten together with Jill. And now, well up into my thirties, pushing forty, this young twenty-something beauty, and a beauty obviously with brains, if she was at UC, looked as if she were ready to reel me in and show me what I had missed all during my high school and college years; even most of my grad years.

But she swept away my total and complete awkwardness with a single toss of her head, expertly throwing her hair back in place with a long-practiced and graceful motion. And I knew at that point that it didn't matter what I did or didn't do. This was her train, and she would conduct affairs from departure to arrival.

All I had to do was climb aboard.

"And then," she continued, not missing a beat, "we started in on issues of *Tin House*, and there you were! Well," she said, as if gathering steam, stoking the story until it blazed bright, with the energy to ride the narrative as far down the rails as need be, "you became the class favorite, instantly, just like that," she snapped her fingers as she said it. "All the stories are so good."

"I'm torn, you know," saying it as if it was the most delicious feeling in the world, to be so torn. "We have to do an assessment of the one piece we consider the best. I'm thinking, probably, 'Fat Elvis Kills.' It's *so* amazing." She beamed. I'd swear her eyes literally sparkled at this point, though physiologically I suppose that's a bit of an impossibility.

But she wasn't done. Both her hands now wrapped around mine. I felt myself lean forward, pulled into her eyes, and my heart beat faster. I tried to calm myself down a bit. She licked her lips, and I forgot about the whole calming myself down thing. While still holding both my hands in hers, she began to gently stroke my fingers with one hand.

"How do you do it?" she asked, her mouth staying slightly open after the words left. Slowly, her tongue came out, and, even more slowly, she touched the tip to her top lip, licked inward, then pressed her lips slightly together before opening them up again to reveal an inviting smile.

Though I heard the question, it didn't really register. For some reason, I found the new moisture on her lips to be fascinating.

She let me hang for a second; maybe to see if I completely belonged to her, or if it'd take a little more stroking of my ego. Then she pressed on, probably deciding a little more stroking never hurt anyone.

As if she had been a naughty girl, mischief in her voice, she said, "I've already read 'Renunciation.'" She paused for a moment. Then, changing persona as if switching out accessories, she squealed, like a high school girl that has just told her friends the school quarterback had asked her out, "*The Paris Review*! You're in the goddamn *Paris Review*! My God!" she declared, "and so soon on the heels of the *New Yorker*!" Her eyes went wide. "How is that even possible?" But then she took a moment and regained her composure a bit. "I'm taking 'Renunciation' to class on Monday, and syllabus be damned! I've already emailed all the students. Hot off the press this week, into the hallowed halls of academe the very next!"

The next thing surprised me. Maybe because I never thought of my writing having consequences. But her tone veered toward the serious as she said, "'The Divine Service,' 'Damnable Lies,' 'Renunciation'—they've really helped me grow up. *You've* helped me grow."

She let that settle in, then she continued. "Church is just so much bullshit. I guess I still hung onto all the little warm fuzzy feelings I'd had when my parents took me to church when I was little. When I moved here, I quit going every Sunday, just every now and then." A look of what—victory?—flashed from her eyes.

"But I know now, thanks to you," she said, squeezing my hand again. "I see what all that religious mumbo-jumbo is. Now, instead of slowly sliding away, I'm taking control. Marching away, with purpose. Because I *see*! Because of you."

She closed her eyes, took a breath, held it, then let it out slowly. She did it a second time, as if in a meditative state. Her eyelids raised, and she shook her head as if in disbelief, as if emerging from darkness, and I had been her light.

I started to feel uncomfortable. I'd just written the pieces. I never thought that anyone would take them seriously enough to make any kind of significant change in their lives. And I didn't know how to think about what she had told me. But, then again, a part of me was proud, in a strange—and now I think wrong—way. My writing had made a difference.

But before I could really weigh the consequences of my action, she squeezed my hand again—really hard. It probably seemed to her that my mind had wondered off. When I looked at her, she again, slowly, licked her lips and smiled. Unless I was completely stupid, she planned on letting at least some of her class mates know she had screwed a famous writer over the weekend.

My mind all of a sudden became totally devoid of any notion of consequences, with my writing or with this girl. A strong impulse within me urged me to just push along. I didn't fight it.

"Can I buy you another drink?" I found myself asking her. I still didn't know exactly what to say, but I thought I could do at least that much. Maybe a drink, then perhaps dinner; at Orly's. Then a trip to my place. Or hers. She might be more comfortable in her own place. It'd been a long time since I'd lived in grad student housing. I could see us, going at it like animals, on the third floor of an old building that still had hardwood floors and ten-foot ceilings, plaster coming off the wall, a grad student quality bed that would make enough noise that the people below would know exactly what was going on. But they probably wouldn't find that as interesting as the other sounds; in my mind, this girl had to be a pretty enthusiastic screamer.

"I'd love one," she said, giving me a little half-smile to let me know I was on the right track, doing the right thing. No, she'd make sure the train arrived at the station. She was the most beautiful conductor I had ever seen.

I turned toward the bar and raised my hand to catch the attention of a waitress. The first thing I noticed was that the devil was nowhere to be seen.

The second thing I saw was Jill, headed straight for me.

At first, I thought perhaps she had seen someone else; maybe a friend she had come to meet. Then the wild thought of ducking under the table came to me, but I wasn't quite sure how that would be perceived by my newfound admirer. And Jill would have seen me anyway, so if she was intent on talking to me, I'd have to crawl back up from under the table. Maybe she just wanted to say "hello." Maybe the roof would fall on me and put me out of what was, I was certain, my impending misery. I quiet groan escaped my lips as I looked into the eyes of my groupie.

I guess it was my demeanor; maybe she was a killer at reading body language. But she knew something was up, and already the sparkle had faded from her eyes.

12

"Hi," I said feebly as Jill stood by the edge of the table. I didn't even notice when my young admirer had withdrawn her hands. Having nothing better to do with them, I kind of threw them up in the air and said, "What are you doing here?"

"Oh, just relaxing a little after work," she said, "though I've heard more polite questions." I guess I hadn't been too gracious in my greeting.

Then, with the most unpleasant smile I've ever seen, she turned her attention to the woman across from me and asked, "And who's your friend?"

"Eh," I said, frantically trying to remember what she had told me. I knew she had said her name, but for the life of me I couldn't remember it. And it wasn't my fault—if she had come on more slowly, given me a chance to find my feet, I wouldn't have been so swept away. Her fault, I decided; pathetic, but that's what I thought.

"Mindy," she said, leaving off her last name, though I was pretty sure she had told me. Then turning the tables on Jill, Mindy frosted her smile as much as possible and asked, "And who are you?"

"Jill," she said, "Jill *McFarland*."

UC girls are smart. She was gone without so much as a "goodbye."

"Timmy," she said, knowing that pet name drove me crazy, mostly because only my mother ever used it, and then only when she was upset with me about something. "Robbing the cradle? Has it come to that?"

I got defensive. "She's a grad student at UC, fully grown. Not that it's any of your business."

I was getting ready for a fight.

But she didn't want to; instead, she slid in across from me, reached over, and familiarly patted my hand. It didn't send shivers through me as when Mindy had reached over and took control, but Jill's touch did feel comforting. The anger dissipated as her hand stopped its patting and rested comfortably on mine.

"Actually," she said, now looking a little embarrassed, "I had stopped by here for a drink before coming to see you." She looked at me as if trying to assess something, like a doctor giving you the once over to see if there's any quick and apparent reason for some malady.

"Oh?" I asked. I was intrigued. We didn't talk much, so I was surprised. In fact, we were still married; she didn't file for divorce after she left me, and I never really wanted to. Maybe she was too Catholic and me too lazy—too inert, too uninvolved in aspects of my life. At least, as I remembered it, that how Jill had characterized me, an armchair psychologist's assessment as she made her way from the armchair to the door. Her presence hadn't graced the armchair or the door since that last day.

She had left, taking only the things she could carry in one trip, sending professionals to gather up what she couldn't. She had kept her own banking account and her own job, even after I had made a bundle. And she never asked for anything, though I did try to offer. She once said, "That's the least part I want from you." I never really knew what she meant.

"I know we split up on bad terms," she said, deciding to have her talk with me here rather than coming over to my place, apparently, or trying to find another mutually agreeable setting. "But that doesn't mean I don't care for you." She took a deep breath, then plunged into what she meant to say.

"I'm worried about you, Timmy," she said. "I just want to know that you're okay."

"Well," I said, a little confused, "Why wouldn't I be okay?"

"First of all," she said, her voice becoming a little sarcastic, "there's your obvious bad taste in women."

"Hold on," I said, again quickly becoming defensive, "She came on to me, not the other way around. I was just sitting here minding my own business."

"I can well imagine that," she said, again sarcasm coming out in a way that didn't help our conversation. How quickly we were settling back into patterns developed over our last few months of life together.

"Look," I said, sitting up in my seat, pulling my hand back from hers, rather roughly. "I know you don't think much of me, but I'm not quite as useless as you think." I then paraded, and paraded really is the right word to use, my string of recent achievements before her, each one a club to hit her over the head, as if to say, "See, I can write, I am good for something."

She sat there and let me crow for a while. Then a tear slipped down her face.

"I'm sorry that I've made you feel so badly about yourself," she said. "I think my own insecurities, and trouble with my folks, made me jump all over you when there was nothing really wrong with you. It was me. *I* was all wrong."

Then she began to cry in earnest.

"I'm sorry for what I've done," she finally said, pulling herself together. I had nothing to say—I was stunned.

"Actually," she said, the corners of her lips turning up a little, "I have read all you've written, at least I think I have. Even the hot-off-the-press *Paris Review* piece." She paused for a minute before she said, "They're all good, really good."

I smiled back at her and reached over and took her hand again. "Thank you," I said.

But then she looked at me, drop-dead serious, and said, "But they're not you."

Not me? Not me? How could she say that? Finally making a mark, and she was saying it was not me. Because I was too stunted? Too little of soul? Too not what she expected? I again pulled my hand back, words choking me, all of them that I wanted to say, but none of them coming out. I had a hard time breathing.

She saw I was upset and tried again to take my hand, but I wouldn't let her. So she simply brought her hands back to herself, laid them in her lap, and again stated, "They're not you."

I finally blurted something out. "What in the hell do you mean, not me?"

A demur look settled on her face, a primness, a properness, and a shyness, as if not wanting to speak out of turn. But she did finally speak.

"Those pieces are jaded," she said, the words coming out barely above a whisper. "They bring out the worst, make everything seem bad. They're so condescending to—well—to everybody, to all the characters, as if you're sitting above them all, judging them." She thought a moment more then said, "Timothy, they're mean spirited, all of them, spiteful, and whatever else you are, you're not mean."

I'd never thought of them as mean; at least not entirely mean. Were they? I slumped down in my seat, rubbing my head. Were these stories really mine, or the devil's? I really didn't think of them as spiteful as I wrote them, just true, true in a raw, unprocessed way. But not mean. Now that she had said it, though, I could see what she meant. I put my head down on the table and banged it once, none too gently, for good measure.

"And I worry about other things, too," she said. I pulled my head up to listen.

"I've got some friends who go to Orly's. You've seen them." I nodded. On more than one occasion, over the usual Monday night dinner with the devil, I had seen some of the old crowd, people we had known when we were a couple.

"They say it's always Monday, our night. Remember?" she asked. And then I did remember. Jill and I always went out on Monday nights when we first dated because they ran specials that were cheaper than anything you could get the rest of the week. Quiche, actually. They ran a quiche special on Monday nights.

"Remember how we'd go on Mondays, you'd get the quiche, I'd get a salad and water." She let out a little laugh. "You never seemed to figure things out."

"What do you mean?" I asked.

"Timmy," she said, laughing a little harder now, "You lived with me for years! You know I can eat like a horse, and I'm not that keen on salad."

"Oh, that's right!" I said, surprised that I had never thought of that before.

"Do I have to spell it out for you?" she asked, reaching over now and laying a hand on my arm. "I liked you, you liked me. You were poor but trying to take me out. You got the cheap quiche. I got the cheapest thing possible—a side salad and water." She laughed again and asked, "You really had no clue?"

I laughed too. "As you know," I said sheepishly, "I'm not always terribly observant when it comes to stuff like that."

"I know," she said, a familiar grin popping up on her face. But it almost immediately faded.

"It isn't just the stories that worry me, you know" she continued. "My friends saw you at Orly's. They'd call, I'd ask questions and find out what was up. Always Monday night. You always getting a quiche, then having the waiter serve salad and water." She stopped for a minute, as if getting herself ready—or me—for the final revelation.

"Timmy, if you missed me, you could have called. I would have come. We could talk. And maybe I could have called, too. I missed you. But I wouldn't do it; not until now. I'm sorry I waited."

My head swirled in confusion. To hear the words she spoke made my spirit soar. I still loved her; I knew that. Maybe we could make it work. But I was missing something in her telling of the story. Why would me eating dinner with someone, even if it was on the same night and the same thing as when we dated, send her into such a tizzy?

I found out.

Though sometimes a bit dense, I can finally get to the bottom of things, if I try hard enough and am so inclined. I thought my head would explode.

Her friends had seen no one with me—ever. The waiter had seen no one with me—ever. And Jerry, the manager who fired probably a decent waiter because of me—had never, ever, seen anyone.

I never thought the devil ate much; I ordered that damn salad for him, but he never did much more than play with it, I thought. Turns out, he never even touched it, more than likely. He just twirled his fork around to make it look like he was eating.

What a moron. That's what everyone must have thought. Poor Timothy off his rocker, mad with heartbreak over his lost love.

And, as a matter of fact, I was heartbroken—but I certainly was not trying to "recreate" the happy times. I'd kept my heartbreak to myself. Only I knew its depth. What Jill described, however, made me sound pathetic as well as emotionally miserable.

We talked some more. It was good. But she ended up going home, with no more than a promise that we'd talk again. She wouldn't even let me get her a cab or walk her home. She could be that way, fiercely independent.

So I started my walk home. Then, all of a sudden, I heard singing. After months of living with the devil, I had studied Wagner, bought the *Ring* cycle, at least gotten acquainted with the parts—especially the third part of the four, which had lots of tenor singing. All the while, I also picked up a little more German, so I wasn't always in the dark about what the devil (so to speak) was going on about. I knew, as I heard that familiar tenor voice, that the devil was walking along singing some of Siegfried's lines.

Brünnhilde lebt!
    Brünnhilde lacht!
Heil dem Tage,
    der uns umleuchtet.

He kept singing it over and over again; I looked around, trying to find him. And then I realized he had begun to change

Brunnhilda's name to BrunnJILLda. God, he always thought he was so clever. I had no trouble translating the simple verses.

BrunnJILLda lives!
BrunnJILLda laughs!
Hail the day
that shines around us!

Then, as I finally spotted old Nick, the verse changed:

Sie ist mir ewig
ist mir immer

The devil himself switched to English as we pulled up alongside each other.

She is mine forever,
Always mine.

Then he let out a belly laugh.

"Funny, isn't it," he said. "Here Siegfried thinks he's found his true love—she lights up his life." He morphed into Debbie Boone, but only for a moment, just enough to get out the first few words of the chorus to "You Light Up My Life," a song finally done to death at weddings, what little life it ever had beaten out of it by lounge lizards masquerading as chapel crooners.

"But the thing is," he continued, talking excitedly, as if he were letting me in on some big secret, "you've got all this talk about forever and always, and then you get that great tragic ending—Siegfried gets stabbed in the back, Brunnhilda rides her horse into the flames of a funeral pyre." He actually threw his head back and laughed. "Wagner may not have quite grasped the nuances and depth of the Norse stories, didn't grasp their true spirit, but I think he was probably on to something when it comes to the tragedy humans call 'love.'"

He stopped to give me a chance to respond. I remained silent. He shrugged his shoulders and took another tact.

"Some woman, eh? She wanted you, you know. That's part of the territory that comes with being both a famous and a serious writer. Keep hanging around a place like UC and the only lonely nights you'll have are the ones you want."

I still didn't say anything. I tried my best to give him a smoldering look, but I think that sort of thing has to come naturally and can't be forced.

"Come on, Timothy, cheer up! I know you'll have no lady companionship tonight, but you now know you can have it when you want. And hey," he said, looking all puzzled, "what's up with Jill? She pretty much spoiled what could have been an eye-opening experience for you tonight, yet she offered nothing in return for effectively nixing it."

I turned on the devil and quietly said, "If you don't mind, I'd rather discuss this back in the apartment, where no one will be around to certify my insanity." I huffed, or a least tried to; I may have ended up just blowing air into the devil's face. Of course, I decided it didn't matter because there really wasn't a face there anyway.

I tried storming back to the apartment, but mostly I winded myself and probably looked to the impartial observer like nothing more than a couch potato slouch out on January 1 for his first (and last) real day of exercise.

As soon as the door closed, I started yelling. "You made a fool of me!"

He simply laughed. "Timothy, I just wanted to make you feel comfortable. Nobody likes eating alone, but there was no reason to pay good money for something that wasn't going to be eaten." Taking on a hurt look, he said, "I was just trying to do you a favor. So shoot me. I was playing the cheap date."

I snorted. With less hurt and more edge, he said, "Besides, you were the one who always suggested we go eat on Mondays. Maybe the problem's not with me—I was just along for the ride—maybe it has to do with you." He took on his Sigmund Freud face. "Actually, is there some attraction between you and me that, somewhere inside, touches a nerve, a place, where Jill resides? Do you find that you have the same sort of feelings for me that you had for Jill? *Verrry* interesting."

When I didn't laugh, he turned back into JFK Jr.

"Look," he said, all businesslike. "Maybe I just gave you more credit than I should have. I always figured you knew the only place I could be was in your head. Think man, think," he emphasized, "did you get all the way through most of a PhD program in the history of theology without realizing what a big deal incarnation is?" His eyes bugged out, as if caught by total surprise. "Incarnation is no snap-of-the-finger sleight-of-hand trick, Timothy. Besides the difficulty," he sniffed, "do you have a clue how disgusting the thought of putting on flesh is for a purely spiritual being? It even stinks for humans, if you believe some of the things my good friend Origen wrote—and did. No thanks. And it'd cramp my style. I can't literally be everywhere at once—oh no, big guy reserves that right for himself, though he could share if he wanted to—but I can be a lot of places. If I incarnate, I'm stuck in one place."

He now appeared as the injured party, as if I were trying to do him harm by stuffing his spirit into some shabby hand-me-down body.

And now that he had mentioned it, he was right. I should have known better; should have realized that he was in my head—how else could he have known so much about me?

He then flashed a boyish grin—full of mischief but not a touch of spite. "Besides," he said, "if you stop and think about it, it's kind of funny."

Despite myself, a bit of a smirk crossed my face.

"Yeah, I suppose so," I said, thinking maybe it was a little funny—although it'd be funnier if it had happened to someone else. Between the embarrassment for being so naive about the incarnation (or was I really so vain as to think the devil would incarnate just to come after me?) and finally seeing the humor in it, I relaxed. A mistake, but I didn't see it at the time.

"Now, my dear Timothy," the devil said, taking a seat and leaning back, nice and comfy, gathering an air of comradeship and concern about him, "Let's talk about Jill."

13

Believe it or not, the conversation about Jill started out with a lecture on John Calvin. I think the devil may have just been showing off again.

"You know Calvin's theology?" the devil asked, placing the finger tips of his hands together, his chin tucked in and resting lightly on top of the thumbs, his index fingers lying gently against the tip of his nose. The same exact pose that my dissertation advisor had the habit of taking when asking me a question that he thought I didn't know how to answer. He was usually right.

So was the devil.

"Not really," I said. I had concentrated on early Christian thought, took exams in some other periods, but mostly bypassed the sixteenth century. Maybe it was that my strangely warmed Methodist heart couldn't take the iron-fisted theology of the sixteenth century—too many people dying (and killing) for the cause of proper doctrine. Too much of a severe Augustinianism run amok. I hadn't the stomach for it.

"You didn't even read the *Institutes*?" the devil asked, incredulity underscoring each word.

"Yes, of course," I snapped, "everybody has to read at least some Reformation materials to get through the general survey courses on Christian thought." He made me feel stupid—not unlike my dissertation committee, two of whom did so out of spite, the other one, my advisor, out of disappointment.

"My God, man!" Then he cocked his head, a sly smile slithering across his face. He was in the mood for a game. "Funny how those two nouns continually pop up next to each other." Then his tone turned professorial. "Timothy, name the most important theological treatise ever written that has God and man side by side in the title."

Then he began to whistle the damned "Jeopardy" tune.

I threw up my hands in frustration, casting a look that I hoped would, if not kill, seriously wound.

My thirty seconds were up. The devil answered his own question. "*Why God Became Man*, by Anselm, I think you should know, 1098. In the original Latin—*Cur Deus Homo*."

"I know that," I said, peevish that I had been so far gone from real theological study that my mind was stuck in English. If I had been at the top of my game, in the middle of my PhD work, I would have gotten the right answer in half a second.

The devil mused a bit. "Man, I loved working with that guy."

"You helped Anselm?" I asked. I should have known.

"Of course," the devil replied. "What a perfectly logical system he set up. The way things ought to work. That's what I do, you know. Keep throwing up to his Highness—using his own handiwork—how things ought to work, if there were any real sense to existence. Anselm did me proud; made things very sensible. Practically bound the will of God to divine properties of justice and love." Then a rude sound came from the devil as he continued, "For all the good it did. Sir Know-It-All should have been embarrassed as *hell*," he said, "this ant of a creature Anselm sketching out a real religious framework, complete with a logic and rules, me always helping him keep his eye on the prize—a perfect paradigm. But no," The devil sighed. "I keep trying, for all the good it does."

"Fun time's over, though," the devil said, getting back to the subject. And he did think of it as fun—little things you'd say, like "My God, man," then going off on it, like it was the funniest thing in the world to point out trivia, little ironies, anything that he thought would make him look clever. A lot of the time, it was kind of funny; just not as funny as he thought. But I almost always got a kick out of him; he was funny just by trying to be so funny.

"Back to Calvin, so we can properly understand Jill," the devil said.

"So, what's Calvin go to do with Jill?" I asked.

"Everything," he said. "Calvin was a great man, you know, a great thinker. A good student."

I didn't question the devil here. I disliked what little I knew of Calvin's theology enough to think that maybe it was the devil behind it all.

"Another clear mind," the devil continued. "You know, he once preached over two hundred sermons on the book of Job. Ended up with a brilliant hypothesis—that there is a righteousness of God by which even the angels of heaven can be judged and found wanting." The devil laughed. "I like that. They're nothing but a bunch of toadies anyway."

I assumed part of his dismissal of the heavenly chorus was the fact that they chose to stay put rather than follow him.

"Anyway, Monsieur Calvin, as I always called him, had an eye for human weakness. What a doctrine!" the devil said, as if in awe. "And I didn't really have much to do with it, just a point of clarification here, a little punching up the logic there."

"The total depravity of the human race, that's what I'm talking about," the devil declared. "The notion that, even in the best act, sin lays at the heart of it somewhere. The clear-headed view that there is, in point of fact, no such thing as a pure, selfless act of goodness, at least where humanity is concerned."

He let that sink in for a minute.

"Don't be blinded, don't be played for a fool, my dear Timothy," the devil said, his voice hardening, his features taking on the appearance of a battle-tested warrior. Immediately I knew—the devil was ready for a fight: against God? against Jill? against me? All three? I wasn't sure.

"Think about it," he said, his voice sharp as a razor, ready to cut away any objections that might be voiced. "Who called you a scrub tree in the great forest of life? Who berated you for being stuck, unable to grow, to move on? Who tore away at your self-esteem, all because she, in her own words, couldn't stomach your continual whining about being a real writer? And who walked out on you, all because you had the good sense to keep Shrineland from coming into existence?"

"Who, Timothy, *who?*"

I thought about Jill, how she looked sitting across from me, concern on her face, care in her touch. I didn't think the devil had it right, not quite.

"I don't know," I said, "she seemed pretty sincere to me."

"Ha!" he laughed, and his voice shook the room, or at least it did so in my hearing of it. "Sincere? Timothy, *Timothy*, think! The executioner is sincere as he swings the axe, but I can't believe that sincerity is worth much to the poor sap who's head is severed from his body." He paused a second, then added, "Or for the patsy whose heart is ripped from his chest."

And all of a sudden, all my feelings for Jill swelled up inside me. Yes, there were the feelings of love, care, and compassion; but there was also the hurt, the anger, the despair caused by our breakup. I saw two images—the Jill who sat across from me in concern, and the Jill who had stormed out of my life, throwing deprecations at me as she left that went straight to my heart. The devil was right—she had ripped my heart out, or at least she had tried to do so.

But there was still the good.

"Yes, that's it, Timothy," the devil said, a glint in his eye. I think he thought he was reeling me in, the fresh catch of the day. "What's in your head, that's what Calvin was talking about. Not black and white, right or wrong, good or evil. It's never either/or with humans, always both/and. And the good and bad are so mixed up together there's no separating them out." He let that sink in. "For Calvin," he continued, "it's not that there's no good, there's just no good enough."

He thought he had me here. And maybe he did, for a while.

"Good enough for what?" I asked.

"Why, there's no such thing as a person good enough for God; not even good enough for another human being. Every man or woman who has ever sucked in the air of life has one center—the big 'I,' the ego, me, mine—and everything else is peripheral."

"I still think love makes a difference," I said, wanting to defend Jill—hell, defend myself, my species—against the devil's accusations.

The devil rolled his eyes. "Okay, mister sentimental gift book writer," the devil said, each word an arrow in my heart. "Love makes a difference. Grand discovery."

Next thing I knew, John Lennon sat in my apartment, singing "All You Need Is Love." He kept hammering away at the chorus, over and over again until I thought I'd go crazy.

I think the devil knew I was fast approaching a snapping point, because he finally changed back to Jr. "Ah, the summer of love," the devil said. "Guess love didn't stop that bullet from taking John, did it?"

"God!" I exclaimed. His face lit up as I said the word. "You always twist things around."

"No," he replied, calm as could be. "The God you just referred to is the one who has twisted things around—made all you humans think there's meaning at the core of existence, a hidden purpose in it all. The notion that love overcomes all, when it's never done a thing for most people except give them a reason to pursue their biological drives with some seeming sense of decency. I see clearly. Every time *you* try to explain away tragedy, or look for the good amidst terrible calamity, or try to pretend that you have some concern for the world at large, or the mass of humanity, or even your family, wife, brother, sister, son, daughter, in such a way that you're not looking for something in return—*that's* twisted."

"Timothy," he said, his voice moving from calm to seductive, soothing, inviting. "Look, look with your special gift, your writer's eye, at what this situation is really all about."

He smiled, almost a rueful smile, a little bit of regret slipping from the corners of his creased eyes, a wistfulness escaping as a small sigh from his lips. Thinking back, this guy was good.

"I'm sorry that I've been pedantic about all this. Really, you've outgrown most of what I can do for you. Maybe one or two tips, really, is all that's left for me to impart, to help you find your real self."

A slight cough sounded, almost as if covering up some embarrassment.

"You see, I've come to really like you. It's fun hanging with you. We work well together. But in this regard, I have overstepped the boundaries. I should be here to listen to you think your way through your feelings toward Jill, not try to cram my point of view down your throat. I'm sorry."

I said he was good—good enough that he had me eating out of his hand. I believed him.

"Tell you what," he said, rising from his seat, heading toward the door. "You do what you do best, and I'll leave you to it."

"What do you mean, exactly?" I asked, falling into his trap.

"Why, I leave you with yourself, to explore, to plumb the depths. Sit down and reflect, think, feel. And then write. There's no better guide to your true affections than you yourself. You have the knowledge; you have the experience; and I know you have the will."

I stood there pondering what he meant; wondering if I really had become that person he described—in other words, if he thought me a real honest-to-goodness writer, one of the great ones.

And after just a moment's thought, I realized that he was gone.

I found myself drawn to the computer. I ran my hand across the screen, and then I placed my fingers on the keyboard. It felt absolutely right, as if from birth I had had letters at the beck and call of my finger tips, waiting to be moved into lines, lines that, though simply black marks on a white screen, somehow or another remade the universe each time I arranged those few little letters—only twenty-six, yet the key to the cosmos, if punched in the right order. And I had the gift of order, the sight to bring it off.

A joining, cybersex in the truest sense of the word, unsullied by graphics or reference to body parts and functions. A coming together of mind and spirit and heart with the letters and words, a coupling that produced an eternal progeny: literature that would speak forever to all who had the nobleness of soul to read and understand.

I had never had such an intense experience before in my writing; as if it had all been foreplay before; now I would no longer be virgin. A virile writer. All I had to do was start and work to climax. A sweet loving, that's all that was required.

And so I began to type.

And the devil was right—or so it seemed at the time. Images flew through my mind at first, but then they slowed down, turning icy, frozen in place. I examined them. I wove words into shapes, into attitudes, into characters. The affections, they became a masterpiece of nuance, never entirely good, never entirely bad, only true, real, substantive.

Once again, I worked through the night. A lover who could not get enough. An initiate who, though exhausted, ached for more of the delight that only came by the union. I melded into oneness, my thoughts and language, producing the comely children that would inhabit their own private world of the story.

But as all such things must end, at the break of dawn, light pouring in through the window, I finished. Satisfaction rode my breath as I exhaled in a final, shuddering gasp.

All that was left was to go back and title the piece.

There was no doubt. "Love's Price" rode the title page like a knight on a steed, sure of his path to glory.

One final touch. I put the manuscript in an envelop addressed to my agent with a letter saying that he should send the piece to the place that would pay the most. Now, most agents don't deal with short story placement. But mine knew he was on the verge on closing a major deal on a novel, so I figured he'd take the challenge.

Then I was done. I placed the 9 x 12 bundle of truth on my desk to mail later. Exhaustion nipped at my heels, and so I made to go to bed. But the doorbell rang.

The aggravation faded pretty quickly upon seeing Agnes, the woman who had been helping me keep the apartment clean for some years now, standing outside, waiting to be invited in. I had forgotten the day of the week—cleaning day. I told her that I had worked all night and was going to sleep, so she could skip my bedroom for the week but go ahead and do everything else—I was so tired I didn't think any noise would bother me.

But before heading off for dreamland, I let her know that I had placed her money on the desk and to be sure and pick it up before she left. I felt generous, having done so much good work, so I left an extra ten for her. She deserved it; she always did a great job.

And I was right—the noise didn't bother me. I fell asleep almost immediately, as if anesthetized. I didn't kick around much; I didn't actually dream any that I remember. Just a long, long sleep, as if I had almost forgotten how to wake up, it went on for so long. When I did finally rouse myself, a fog of forgetfulness surrounded me, as if the day before had been shrouded from my sight as if it were its own blessed isle of Avalon—I knew it was there, just not where, just not the particulars. And I found I didn't really care.

14

June had broken over Chicagoland like a gift from heaven—seventy-five degrees, wispy clouds, dry air, a nice little breeze. The devil had been with me, what? Nine-plus months? I found I spent little time with other companions, mostly just him and me, talking about the ways of the world, me writing. It should have felt stifling, thinking back, but it wasn't. For the most part, we got along. He kept pushing me to see the world more and more as he saw it. I resisted at times, went along at others.

But the day had come when he decided it was time to fish or cut bait. To really, finally, join him or not. I think he thought he had won, but he made a terrible mistake. I had no idea going into that Sunday in June that it would be the last day I spent serious time with him. There was only one other, very short visit after that.

A beautiful morning greeted me. The sun shone over Lake Michigan like some beneficent, good-natured Greek god, glad to have his chariot out and riding. I made some coffee, started to sit down at the computer and write a little, but I decided not to. I was going to take it easy for the day.

I looked forward to the afternoon. In a fit of planning—something we didn't do all that much—the devil and I decided to go to Oak Park for the afternoon. The first suburb due west of Chicago, Oak Park carried the charm of an old-fashioned suburb, near but not in the city, not frightened of the urban in the same way the outlying suburbs were. It had been home to Frank Lloyd Wright and Ernest Hemingway, and the entire village exuded a sophistication that befit such inhabitants. Lots of trees, grand old houses, interesting apartment buildings. A great place to visit, and probably an even better place to live. I had some friends out that way, and they lived pleasant lives there.

First stop, we were going to the Village Players, the local theater, to watch a Tennessee Williams play. The devil could barely contain his excitement. He thought it'd be a great thing for me to see. "A brilliant play," he said, "much more so than the critics think. I'll coach you on what to look for, the nuances. Comedy? Yeah! But one that tells the very sad story of the human situation. What can you do but stand back and laugh, if you're going to get anything at all out of this existential cesspool you folks think of as life."

I assumed the devil had had a hand in crafting the play, but I didn't go there. Sounded innocuous enough. "A Lovely Sunday for Creve Coeur," played at three that afternoon. "Remember your French, Timothy," the devil teased. "Creve Coeur, you know what it means?"

"Broken Heart," I replied.

"It's not just a 'burb near St. Louis," the devil added. "It's the world."

Still, it would be fun. We would go see the play, I'd listen to him lecture me about it, I might argue with him, I might not, depending on my mood. But he always had interesting—if obnoxious—things to say, and he put an ironic twist on about everything, doing so with a humor that could be deadly.

Afterwards, a walking tour of the city in the late afternoon. And the day, judging by its beginning, anyway, would be perfect for it.

Early morning became late morning. I had cleaned up my breakfast dishes and had just put away the frying pan when I heard a knock on the door.

"Come on in," I yelled. I turned and saw the devil in the same black pinstripe suite in which he had first appeared. Sometimes I would think, "He's not really there, he's just in my head. Why does he even bother with the charade of knocking?" But most of the time I went along with the illusion—though when we were in public I no longer acted as if someone sat immediately across from me, and I no longer ordered meals for him. But I still ate, and we still talked, though in a more discreet way, for my part.

He went to his favorite chair and sat down. "Timothy, dear boy, how are you today?" he asked.

"Great," I said, and I meant it. It would be a good day, I was sure.

"Well, there's the spirit," he said. "Looking forward to our little romp into suburbia?"

"Indeed," I said. In fact, I couldn't explain it, but for some reason I couldn't wait to get out and about, start on our adventure.

"Well, we've a few hours on our hands before we have to go," the devil said. "How about a little TV? Reality TV, if you like. May give you some insight into the play we're going to see."

And then, with a wave of his hand, images appeared on the screen.

Over the past few weeks, the devil had begun to show me things on TV that astounded me. Things, I think, meant to impress me. His connections ran all the way up to the top in businesses, politics, churches, show biz. Ministers, priests, presidents, dictators, actors, writers, little people, big people—the devil's influence was widespread. He told me how he kept up with them all through devil-cam—sometimes even talked with them through the TV screen. He'd done that for me once or twice, more like a parlor trick than anything else, I think, to wow me. It let me know how involved in the world he was, how big the operation stood, and how he played such a central role in creating a workable vision of what the world should be like. One time, I felt overwhelmed by his seeming endless power to sway people. He must have been able to gauge that awe in me, because just as I thought it, he turned from the screen and said to me, "Timothy, you are special. You are in the same league with these folks. All you need is a little help; like I helped them." A pat on the knee might as well have been a pat on a good dog's head, that's how unthinking in my adulation I had become.

But for that Sunday, we watched something else. At the time, it seemed an odd "show." Sad, but not terrible. The devil had opened my eyes to the little things in life that lead to torturous murders of soul. And for my writer's eye, that had been good. Though we sometimes talked of calamity and disaster on large-scale terms—and saw how it played out on the TV—we both knew it was the intimate, personal details of disaster that really speak to the human condition. And that's what we watched that day.

On a tree-lined street, an older lady lived her life out in silence and loneliness. Her husband had been gone for fifteen years, a good man whom she sorely missed. And not long after that, her own personal tragedy struck—a tumor on her larynx. They saved her life but took her voice. She felt too old to learn sign language, and she didn't know whom she would speak to anyway. They had had no children, though she loved children, and her marriage to the dashing young soldier had taken her far from her own family, none of whom she saw anymore. And she was old enough now that it was kind of hard to get around, and longtime friends had either died or moved. The quietness of her life deafened her.

She tried. Tried to reach out a little bit. She had a pastor who saw her occasionally, though the occasions became more and more rare. He encouraged her to meet people, even if it were the people on her street, people who had come in and replaced neighbors she had known for years. It was hard, but she tried.

The failure of it all almost killed her. So maybe she went a little crazy, became too needy. A young couple with a small child, just old enough to crawl around good, moved in across the street. She had greeted them on moving day with an apple pie and a note. Then she tried to make a relationship develop—a few more apple pies translated into holding the little tyke on occasion. But, by and large, these were young people, and they wanted no real part of a friendship with an older lady whom they didn't know, couldn't really talk to without the cumbersome process of reading note after note, and so they became distantly polite.

Then not so polite. She knew they were home the several times she took over pie, but no one came to the door. The friendliness of the waves "hello" took on the rigid turn of hand that spelled duty, and then finally the young people pretended not to see her, and they wouldn't wave at all. For some reason—maybe a good one, maybe not, maybe thought out, maybe not—they had decided they didn't need the old lady, despite the fact that she obviously needed them. But they didn't want the responsibility, and who could blame them? They had their own friends, their jobs, their own little family. They didn't want a drag on their full lives. And it made the old lady sad, and she often cried at night.

"Well," I told the devil, "this is pretty depressing."

He continued to watch the show, fascinated by what was going on.

I sighed. If this is what the play was going to be like, I thought, maybe my enthusiasm had been misplaced. But then the devil came around from his absorption in the small-screen drama and spoke.

"What do you think of this, Timothy?"

"Not much," I said, "just the continuing saga of human apathy."

"Aren't you outraged? Are you so jaded now that no anger boils to the surface, no sense of justice cries out for retribution? Do you know how much it would mean to that old lady if they'd just wave 'hello' now and again?" The devil's questions came quickly, bluntly, as if begging for answers.

"Sad, but it's the same-old same-old," I said.

"Nothing you'd write about?" he asked, seeming particularly interested in my response to something so mundane as to elude good, sharp description.

"Don't think so, not based on what I've seen," I replied. I looked at my watch. It was past one. "We'd better get going. I hate having to rush," I said.

"By all means," the devil said, a look of satisfaction and—what, happiness?—warming his face. "Wonders await us."

We pulled out of the parking garage and headed north on Lake Shore Drive. I had the top down—my one real conceit once I came into money was my convertible, an old, beautifully restored '63 'vette.

Enthusiasm once again filled my lungs. On a clear dry day, the skyline of downtown Chicago, coming up along the lake, is a picture-perfect sight. It was such a day, and there was nothing better than to be out driving, just taking it all in. I finally passed Soldier Field, made my way through Grant Park, and got on Congress, which soon turned into the Eisenhower, I-290. We headed west for several miles then took the off-ramp at Harlem. North a few blocks, and we were at Madison. I turned right, and down the street sat the Village Players building.

I started to pull the car over into a nice shady metered spot when the devil said, "Why not turn north here, and let's park a few blocks away."

"How come?" I asked.

"Well, I think you've been looking forward to getting out and walking, haven't you? Isn't that the idea? A little tour of Perfect Place, USA? See some of the architecture, all that." I ignored the sarcasm.

"Actually, it's a fine idea," I said. "Though we can do the leisurely tour after the play. I don't like to be late."

He just nodded, acquiescing to my every whim, at least appearing to do so.

So we pulled onto a little side street, a residential street, where all the houses sat proudly, as if beckoning back to an earlier time in history, a better time.

The place actually looked a little familiar, but I didn't want to spend a lot of time looking. I had parked about eight blocks north of the theater, almost a mile. I set a reasonable pace, one that had purpose but wasn't rushed.

We made the play in plenty of time. I took in a little of its history from the playbill. A pretty late play, in fact. 1979, I read. Apparently from a time in Williams' life when the magic had left him—the play opened to so-so reviews and followed on the heels of a bonafide failure. I laughed. The play that had bombed had the word "devil" in the title. I showed the devil and laughed, though he just "harumphed" and turned a haughty nose upward.

"Don't ever trust reviewers; or most of the audience, for that matter," the devil finally said, leaning over and whispering to me, as if he were telling me a great big secret. "Believe me, the plays—both the one we're seeing today and the other so-called 'failure' you pointed out to me—hit their intended target. These plays changed lives, but that's not the kind of thing that get's written up in a review, because not much of anyone knows about it—except me."

As I started to respond, he simply placed his fingers to his lips—shush, he was telling me, an all-knowing confidence in his expression. And sure enough, the lights went down. But what did he really know? Just about the lights, or was he hinting at something else? I never got a chance to find out.

The play came and went. A nice production, it was, as was usual for Village Players. I had been there numerous times. Not quite the quality of the big theaters downtown, but an intimacy reigned at Village that was often missing from the larger venues. And the people were good—if not quite good enough for the big show, more than adequate for "village" theater.

We walked out, and the devil left me with my thoughts for a few minutes. I mulled things over—four women, Depression-era St. Louis area. Parts were funny; parts were sad. They were survivors, the four women, still trying to hang on to some shred of a dream of one sort or another. But the women had been shredded themselves in the process, not coming out quite whole.

"What's the heart of the play, my dear Timothy?" the devil asked, finally breaking the silence.

"I don't quite know," I said, not having had the time to really digest the play, thinking I'd probably need to see it—or at least read it—again.

"Very simple," the devil responded, a certainty that brooked no opposition. "Dorothea, the one holding out for true love, giving what shouldn't have been given. She's the heart of this broken-heart play." The devil let out a sigh.

"As usual," he continued, "words so fail at times when a world, or at least one's dream for a world, falls apart. But Williams got it as near perfect as he could."

Dorothea. A teacher who had hopes of marriage with her principal. Her principal, who enjoyed her willingness, used it. The principal at the heart of her dreams. Yet, turns out, he was engaged to another woman. And so Dorothea ends up going out with her roommate's brother. Something she does knowing it's a step down, moving from dream to reality, and one that she would not have chosen for herself.

The devil had given me time to think about Dorothea. He had good instincts. At times like that, he knew exactly when to hold his tongue, when to talk. So, I turned to him, ready to hear what he had to say. He spoke immediately once my attention had fallen on him.

"We must go on, that's all that life seems to offer and demand."

Dorothea had spoken those words, near the end of the play. A resignation, a giving up. On a picnic with her roommate and her roommate's brother, she understood life would be no more, could be no more, than just going on. All it offers. All it demands. That's life.

"There is no big picture, Timothy," the devil said. "Some people get lucky in life; most don't. And even the lucky ones have more damnation in their souls than you can imagine, appearances to the contrary. Nobody wants life exactly the way it is; but nobody can change it."

"Then what's left to do?" I asked.

"Why Timothy, don't you know?" the devil asked, genuinely surprised. "Acknowledge it. And in your case, with your gifts, write about it. Help people to see, really see, what life is all about—a mindless going on. Nothing more. Nothing less. Sartre knew," he said, once again reminding me that he and Sartre had been collaborators. "You got one real choice. Take life for what it is—nothing—or exit stage right."

I nodded my head. For about one minute, the devil had me. But I guess he wasn't all-knowing after all. He had one more trick up his sleeve, meant to seal the deal. Turned out to be a breaker.

15

The devil slowed down, setting a leisurely pace. I was in the midst of thinking about what he had said when, all of a sudden, I had a feeling of déjà vu. I stopped dead in my tracks.

"This looks awfully familiar," I said.

"Well, you've been in Oak Park before; surely you've walked this street at one time or another," the devil said. But the tone of his voice made me think something was afoot; I just couldn't put my finger on it.

Then, all of a sudden, I knew. This was the street—the street from the TV show we had been watching that morning. I looked up the street, then turned around and gave it the once over. The same exact street.

And up about two-thirds of a block, there was the silent house, the old lady with a head full of words but no way to say them. And then I saw her.

She jumped up out of her seat waving frantically across the way. I knew who lived across the street; the young couple who had grown perfectly comfortable ignoring her. She must have been desperate to talk, waving like that, as if the whole world depended on her getting their attention.

Fat chance. Looked like the couple was saying good-bye to their friends. Maybe they'd had a nice afternoon together; maybe lunch; maybe an early dinner. Who knows? But they wore each other's company like an old sweater, completely at ease and cozy with one another.

The young couple had seen their friends to the car. It was sweet; the young man opened his door and his wife or girlfriend slid in through the driver-side door, just far enough over to allow her darling in, sitting close together for a Sunday drive.

Then I saw several things at once. The engine started up, and I saw the man put the car in reverse. All of a sudden, the woman on the outside of the car stopped her waving goodbye and began to look around; and within a split second she became frantic in her searching. Her husband had just turned to head back inside. The old lady across the street began to run across her porch, arms flailing, hoping to get someone's attention. Her foot caught, and I saw her begin to fall.

At the same time, I saw a baby crawl around from the other side of the car—the young couple's baby. That's what the mother had missed all of a sudden. She must have set the baby down and not noticed that the little thing had crawled away.

The car moved backwards. I later learned that I had been helpful, insofar as I could have been. I remember running, trying to get someone's attention, but that's all. They say I called 911 on my cell phone, so the police and ambulance were there in nothing flat. They say I went over to see to the old lady—in pain, unable to speak. Found out later that she had broken her pelvis in the fall; she later died in the hospital, not wanting to live after watching what she did and not being able to stop it.

But all I remember, after starting to run, was screaming. Screaming "stop." I don't know if I yelled it out loud at first, and then it just stayed in my head, or if the whole time I tried to help I punctuated my actions with screaming. One long scream. That's all I remember. Long, and sad, and lonely.

There was nothing the paramedics could do for the baby. Later, as I gave a full accounting to police, after I had calmed down, after the screaming had left my throat and head, I saw the couples again, at the police station. Guilt had destroyed the one couple;

blind rage and hatred had engulfed the other. There would be no more Sunday afternoons together.

But for the then-and-there of it, that terrible Sunday, the people in charge finally said to go home. I started to walk up the street, blindly trying to find my car—it seemed so long ago that I had parked. And then I saw him—the devil stood there, waiting for me.

"Go away!" I said. I couldn't stand the sight of him.

"My dear Timothy," he started to say.

"Get the hell away from me!" I tried to yell, though it came out more as a croak. I had worn my throat raw.

"Calm down, drive home safely," the devil said, putting a patronizing twist on "safely." He started walking away, throwing over his shoulder as he did so, "We'll talk later."

I did make it home. And then I found my way to a bar, trying my best to wash away the images of the day. I never completely succeeded, but I was able to wear them away enough that what remained were only fuzzy pictures of awfulness—better than the razor-sharp preciseness that I thought would excise my heart from my chest.

They knew me at the bar, though they had never known me to get drunk. But, hey, I was the local famous writer—at first hack, now not—and so the barkeep called a cab, and they sent me safely home.

I don't really remember getting into bed, but I did. I didn't get out for a couple of days, except for the necessary trips to the bathroom; though I was so uncaring I didn't quite make it once. Oh well, I figured. Might as well give the apartment the same sort of stench that hovered around my life. And so it went for a while.

The day I got up and decided to enter the world of the living, starting with a shower, that was the last day I saw the devil.

Of course, at first I heard him. I had just stepped out of the refreshingly cold shower I had taken and was in the process of drying myself off when I heard humming coming from the living room—not words, so much, just the humming.

I wrapped my towel around me and stormed into the living room, leaving a little trail of water behind me.

"Ah, wet as a water rat," the devil said, flashing his teeth at me in a huge smile.

"How dare you come in here after what you did!" I said, shaking with rage. It all came back so quickly, so clearly.

"Hmm," the devil replied. "And so what's it going to be, my dear Timothy? Remember what Dorothea said: 'We must go on, that's all that life seems to offer and demand.' Isn't that it? For you? For the young couple who so cavalierly ignored a neighbor in need? If they had just paid attention; had just been a little less practiced in their complete withdrawal from that old woman. They would have seen something was terribly wrong. Brought it on themselves. Will they go on, you think?"

A roar bellowed forth. I thought my head would blow off my shoulders.

"You knew it would happen," I said, spitting the words out with as much vitriol as possible, every syllable an absolute accusation.

"Knew?" the devil said, throwing his shoulders up in a shrug. "Call it a very educated guess. I don't really experience time like you do—all nice and straight and linear. More like a field of relations within overlapping circles. I could see how things were more than likely going to end up, but I wasn't absolutely certain. Free will can always throw things off at the last minute; but not very often, really. Let's just say I was almost certain it would happen."

"And you did nothing!" I whispered, disgust punching the words.

"Me?" he said, as if caught completely by surprise. "Me? You expect me to do something about all the little tragedies of life? You think that's *my* job? Shouldn't you be talking to someone else about that? To his Highness who sees these circles clearer than I do and does nothing? To the brothers and sisters of your kind, the human race? A little compassion would have gone a long ways toward stopping what happened today." Then he laughed an ugly laugh, a dismissive laugh.

"I'm not a goddamned babysitter," he said, witheringly superior in his tone. "I simply show you the truth; looks like you're one of those who just can't handle it." He let that ride for a few minutes, then he added, "Hack."

"What was all this about then?" I asked, despair smothering me now, fighting with the rage, a wet blanket thrown over a hot fire. I thought my insides would burst.

"Education," he said, looking at me for all the world as if I were the stupidest person on earth. "This is it, Timothy," he said, laying down an ultimatum. "I can only help so much, but you finally have to commit. A test. I didn't cause what happened, and I couldn't have done anything about it. The world is what it is; His preciousness won't intervene, you people make a muddle of it all and make it ten times worse for each other, with these ridiculous hopes that one day a chariot from heaven will swoop down and make it all better."

His eyes bored through me at this point.

"Ain't gonna happen, chump," he continued. "If you can see what happened the way I see it, you've passed the test. We can work together from now on. If you can't, we're done. You gotta give me something in return for what I've invested—either that or I've got to cut my losses now." He gave it about ten seconds to sink in, then in a conciliatory tone, he suggested, "Why not sit down at the computer, try to write this up. See what happens. If you can work on this material, you've got it in you to work on anything—all the subjects the little writers avoid, all the insights that belong to the greatest writers, it'll all be yours. Just try writing."

Then he stood waiting. Guns, drums, all loud things, went off in my head. I couldn't hear myself think. I thought maybe I had fallen off the edge, gone crazy. From the top of my head to my toes, the shaking began in earnest. Was it a minute, five minutes, a day? I didn't know. But when it had finished with me, whatever it was inside, I found I had one simple question.

"Why didn't you tell me?" I asked.

"Tell you what?" the devil asked.

"What was going to happen. You said you couldn't do anything to stop it. Physically, that's true, I believe. There's no 'you' there to do anything. But you could have told me, let me decide whether to try and stop it or to simply watch the fallout of consequences, people reaping what they had sown. Wouldn't that decision have told you all you needed to know about me?"

"Timothy," the devil said, this time putting as much seduction in his voice as possible, an invitation almost too strong to resist. "Write."

But I did resist.

I took a step toward the devil. With all the bravado I could muster, I said, "You were afraid of the choice I'd make."

"Timothy," the devil began again, but I cut him off. I kept seeing that poor baby, over and over again in my head. And I didn't stand off and look with the cool detachment of the devil's kind of writer; instead, a weepy emotion moved through me at the thought of what had happened. He'd have called it maudlin. Looking back on it, I'd call it the first shred of real human decency I'd shown in a long time.

And then the rage came, all of a sudden, completely unexpected. A visceral, angry, white righteousness almost blinded me from the inside out as it exploded within me.

"Coward!" I screamed. And maybe it was because I wasn't thinking, because all I could see inside my head was ripping him from head to toe, because my head and heart, body and soul, were all one at that moment—maybe it was for that reason, or for some other, but when I rushed the devil and grabbed him by the shirt collar, I felt something beneath my hands, and a weight as I lifted him up and shook him. So right; it coursed through my very blood how right it was to attack him.

But then, next thing I knew, he had slipped from my grasp—after all, there shouldn't have been anything there to grasp at all—and he wasn't happy.

It was his turn to hurl angry words. He stepped close, nose to nose. His was a cold rage, and I thought I would freeze to death. And then I looked into his eyes as he spoke.

"How dare you, you little piece of mud," the devil spat. "Don't fool with me, or you'll find out how much trouble I can be." Then his eyes turned to liquid pools of black, and I fell through them, through space and time, into the absolute darkness of timelessness. Then, after what seemed—what? An eternity? I don't know. There was no time. It was what it was.

But then a gigantic light spread across my vision, and after a while, as my eyes adjusted, I saw stars, new stars, brilliant white stars, screaming through space—no, creating space itself as they were flung outward. And with space came time, and I knew I watched millennia played out before me in just a few seconds. And then, I was out of the pool. I took a great, gasping breath, knowing I hadn't breathed for—how long? I don't know.

And then the devil stepped back, haughty in his composure, arrogant in his stance.

"It was me, little man," the devil said. "What you saw was me. I was the one who brought forth the light. I was the *angel of light*. I was the one who set this universe ablaze; I was the one who bathed the darkness with light. His plan, sure. But the actual work—me. All me. Him standoffish, as if he couldn't dirty his hands with the real work of creation; the Word whispering in my ear, his inane directions rambling on, as if I needed them. I didn't."

He glared at me and continued, "Insolent fool. You dare call me a coward? I was at the heart of it all, everything. Comprehend?"

Then again he blinded my soul with darkness, and not only did I see the little baby being run over again, but I felt the pain of a world that had one awful thing after another happen to it. And all the bad choices, the wrong decisions, with devastating consequences, they hit me. And then I heard the howls of the damned, screaming in utter despair. Suddenly the light came back, and this time I was blinded, not by darkness, but by light.

A hot and fiery light, it was. And I saw writhing in agony a great host, abandoned indeed by hope, and who knew nothing except the extent of their own damnation.

I was back in the apartment all of a sudden, rubbing my eyes, trying to wipe the horror away.

The devil stood before me, and he had grown. He loomed menacingly over me. He wrapped himself in a mantle of authority, of privilege, of power. He said simply, "So happens to all who cross me." Then there was silence. He dared me to speak.

I realized that, so much more than the little game I thought it was, I was caught up in a much bigger battle, a cosmic one. The blinders of self-love had kept me from seeing what had almost happened. I had been playing with fire—real fire—and my soul stood scorched. The pain of it struck me, and regret enveloped me. But more than that, truth hit me, and with truth I hit back.

Because, as awesome as the devil seemed to be, and as scared as I was, I knew I had hit home. I knew the truth. He in fact was a coward, and a liar.

And so with more assurance than I had ever felt in my life, I stepped forward and pointed my finger at his chest.

"That's great," I said, my rage returning, narrowing to a point, like a laser, ready to penetrate precisely, deeply; so different from my bulldozer rage of a few moments ago, something that had given me the gumption to try to grab hold of the devil and shake him. No, it was sharp now; I wanted to cut through exactly where it would hurt the most. And I did.

"*Was*," I said, "You said it 'was' you that had the power to create in the beginning. You may have been that great angel of light a long time ago, but you're not now. *Was*. Else you wouldn't be wasting your time on the likes of me." I gave that a moment to sink in, then I turned my back on him as I said, "Get out. You're no longer welcomed here." Almost as an afterthought, I added, "Has been."

I thought he'd put up a fight, engage me somehow or another. But he didn't. He left as he had come in—with a song, again from Wagner's *Ring* cycle, again from his favorite of the four works, his beloved *Siegfried*.

Als zullendes Kind
zog ich, dich auf

Well, I had learned enough German and studied enough Wagner to interpret the lyrics in my own way—I might have been, in fact, nothing more than a whimpering, ungrateful child. But the devil himself, he had picked his own part just right, singing the lines of Mime, and I now knew it: he was, in fact, no more than a whimpering, self-pitying dwarf of a figure.

So, he had formed his judgment of me, and I of him. We never spoke again.

16

"Hey," I said, a suppressed grin cracking the nonchalance I'd tried to plaster across my face. "I'm glad you came."

I stood up, waiting for Jill to take her seat across from me. After just a moment's hesitation, she did.

"It's really nice to see you here," I said. It was Monday, and we sat at Orly's. "You don't have to get the salad, you know."

She laughed a little. A good sign, I thought.

She reached into her tote bag and pulled out a manuscript, sliding it my way across the table. In a large and indulgent italic font, the letters across the title page declared: *The Devil Likes to Sing*.

"This is good, Timothy," she said, "though honestly I don't know what to make of it."

After a moment's hesitation, fighting embarrassment, she asked, "Do you expect me to believe it?"

"Oh, no," I said, rather too nonchalantly, too quickly. I took a deep breath. I was trying too hard. "I just wanted to give the contours of my very strange mind—and actions—some outlet."

"Well," she said, fidgeting with the necklace at her neck—she always did that when she was nervous—"I kept thinking that this book was supposed to be some kind of excuse for your actions, or maybe even an apology, or both. But when I could quit thinking about it that way—and quit thinking that it was you who wrote it—I liked it. Quirky fun in some spots, sad in others." Then she let out a little laugh. "People will think you're crazy."

"It's supposed to be fiction," I said, trying again too hard to be convincing when she really didn't need convincing. Of course she read it as fiction. How could I tell her otherwise?

"But only part," she said. "Parts were real, and you know they hurt." Now tears had snuck into the corners of her eyes; she tried to dab them before I noticed, but it was too late.

She straightened up. "There was a sweetness I liked, too, a naivete buried in it, and I always hoped it'd come out, finally, and replace all the dark cynicism. I wasn't sure though, if it would or not."

We sat in silence for a few minutes, awkward, first-date awkward. And maybe this is what that was, the start of a new relationship, a better one.

A waiter came by to take our order. She didn't get the salad.

She drew in a breath and slowly exhaled. I could see she was steeling herself, determined to say something that she thought might be best left unsaid, unsure of the consequences if she spoke. But she went ahead.

"It really hurt my feelings, you know," she said. I knew immediately what she was talking about. "Love's Price," which had taken such a cynical look at Jill's love, my parent's love, at all love, hadn't been misplaced, as I originally thought when I couldn't find it shortly after having written it. Agnes, who had cleaned the day after I finished the story, took it off my desk and mailed it. I always left her money in the same place for her services, and sometimes I laid out extra money and mail—extra money was for her time and for stamps so that she would take things to the post office for me. She told me later that, with me being so tired and going to sleep the way I had, and with me having left her extra money that day, she thought she was supposed to take the manuscript packet down to the post office and send it off.

Of course, it was published almost immediately (in *Harper's*, no less; my agent took my letter seriously about getting as much for it as he could), and I was pretty sure the devil had a hand in making sure Agnes mailed it.

"I know," I said to Jill. "I've already begged my parents forgiveness; they come off worse than you, you know," smiling weakly, hoping that would take a little of the pressure off to explain myself. It didn't.

"It's true, I wrote it," I continued, willing her to believe me but knowing she'd have to decide for herself, her own choice; that free-will bugaboo.

"But you have to believe me," I said, all of a sudden sounding desperate. "I didn't mail it. That was an accident. I don't think I would have really brought myself to send it off. But I was angry and trying to work through some things in my own head. I didn't mean what I wrote, at least not the way it came out."

I looked to see if she was still with me, or if I had already lost her. I saw in her eyes that she was still there.

"Please forgive me, Jill," I said, pouring my heart's sincerity into those few words. I wanted to explain more, but I knew, for the right then and there of it, explanation took a back seat to just trying to bridge the awful chasm I had created between us.

Her eyes sparkled with moisture. "I want to, but it may take some time." Then her hand reached across the table for mine, and very briefly she squeezed my hand as she said, "But I really want to try."

She withdrew her hand but not her presence. We had a very nice evening.

She talked about her work, how *our* friends (I took that as a good sign) had been doing, how they were always asking about me. She had followed the incredible meteoric rise of my serious writing career. We sat and talked at length about some of the things she had tried to tell me at Jimmy's Tavern; and we both agreed that, however good those stories might have been, they weren't me, not really.

She mentioned that her parents had recently received a fairly sizable sum of money, anonymous, and though it wasn't enough to start construction on Shrineland, they did use it to make some repairs—age had begun to take its toll on some of the older shrines.

She looked at me with a question in her eyes. All I replied was that, I had heard, Gyms for Jesus had also received the same amount of anonymous money. She looked satisfied, saying it was very nice of whoever had done that.

The evening began to wind down. As we talked, it became clear we were at least feeling out the notion of getting together again, just to talk, but with the hope that the talk might lead somewhere. She said she missed me, despite everything. I told her I missed her because of everything. She didn't quite know what to make of that; me either, really, but it sounded true when I said it, so it must have been.

"I have some news," I said, sheepishly looking over, gauging her willingness to put the end of the evening off just a little longer.

"Really?" she asked, interested to hear, as far as I could tell. "Good news?"

"I think so," I said. "I've been talking with my publisher directly, though that's driving my agent wild."

"What about?" she asked.

"Well, don't go crazy on me—I'm not going dark side, not like with my short stories. But I am under contract to deliver a few more gift books, and I wanted to take them in a different direction."

"But not toward the dark side of the force?" she asked, listening to me, and encouraging me, and laughing a little with me.

"Oh no, not that," I said, also laughing. "It may sound a little dark side, but it's really meant to be more along the funny side, though funny with a little bite, perhaps."

"What are you working on, Timothy?" she asked, ready to hear where I was headed.

"A new gift book, same format as always," I said. She cocked her head, about to throw out either a question or objection, but I threw up a hand to stop her.

"Your idea, really," I said, waiting for a reaction. Finally, slowly, an eyebrow arched as she asked, "Yes?"

"Remember after the first book, when it was out but we weren't really sure if it would sell? It was a Monday morning, we were getting ready for work, and I was complaining about having to go and wishing I'd get rich and we'd never have to work again. Remember?"

She shook her head. "Not really," she admitted.

"Well, what you said was this: 'Maybe you need to write something about how bad it is to go to work on Mondays—that'd sell millions because that's exactly how every person in the world feels.' And then you hesitated and added, 'Except me. I love going to work.'"

She grinned. She, in fact, did love going to work, which is why she kept it up after we had enough money not to have to worry about a steady check every two weeks.

"Okay, hot shot," she said, "so what are you working on?"

"Ready?" I took my fingers and did a quick drum roll on the table. "*101 Not So Good Things about Monday*."

And even though it wasn't all that funny, we both laughed all the way out of the restaurant. She let me hail a cab for her, then she kissed me on the cheek. I strolled home, singing schmaltzy 70s love ballads the whole way. Even Karen Carpenter songs. It was a test. I never once heard another voice dogging me, mocking the sentiment. Not even my own.

Afterword

This book is a work of fiction. Its setting, however, is not. I lived for a time in Hyde Park in Chicago, as well as in Oak Park, which shares its east boundary with Chicago's west boundary. I should make a few things clear.

In Hyde Park, there was a restaurant named Orly's. After being a fixture there for about thirty years, there is now no "Orly's." As with all restaurants, it had its supporters and its critics. While a student in Hyde Park, I did not often have the money to eat at Orly's. When I did, I ordered the quiche, and I thought it quite good.

There is no St. Augustine Episcopal Church in Hyde Park; the area is served by St. Paul and the Redeemer Episcopal Church, a congregation which ministers to the Kenwood and Hyde Park communities. I have never attended that church. For reasons of my own, I have created the St. Augustine's portrayed in this book, mostly so I could meditate a bit about St. Augustine of Canterbury. I should also note that there is no connection whatsoever between the St. Augustine's of this book and the St. Augustine Episcopal Church in Danville, Indiana, where I gladly worship among people unlike any portrayed in this book's fictional congregation.

I want to emphasize that the members of Timothy McFarland's dissertation committee—sketched out in the briefest of ways in the early part of this work—are *not* based on faculty members at the University of Chicago Divinity School, past or present, in any way.

Jimmy's is how many folks refer to the Woodlawn Tap at Woodlawn and 55th. Jimmy was the barkeep for decades. It is a place where many university folks hang out, along, of course, with others. Do not, however, take my minimal description of the inside at face value (no establishment likes to think of its windows as "grimy"); I've never actually been in Jimmy's. Nothing against the establishment; many of my friends loved it. It's just that I'm not a drinker (a very occasional social drink, but never beer).

The Village Players of Oak Park, Illinois, provided great theater experiences while I lived in Oak Park. The Village Players building stood at 1010 W. Madison Street, and the tradition of theater continues there in the form of the Madison Street Theater. For sentimental reasons, I have retained the old name. This book features a play that, as far as I know, never actually graced the stage of the Village Players.

Of course, no one should take the devil's declarations on Christian history, worship, music, practice, or theology at face value; he is, after all, somewhat biased.